COMPUTERS
IN SOCIETY

JAMES N. HAAG, Ph.D.
Professor of Computer Science and Physics
University of San Francisco

Consulting Editor, Computer Sciences

COMPUTERS IN SOCIETY

The Wheres, Whys, and Hows of Computer Use

DONALD D. SPENCER
President
Abacus Computer Corporation

HAYDEN BOOK COMPANY, INC.
Rochelle Park, New Jersey

Library of Congress Cataloging in Publication Data

Spencer, Donald D
    Computers in society.

    Includes bibliographical references.
    1. Electronic data processing. 2. Electronic
digital computer. 3. Computers and civilization.
I. Title.
QA76.23.S62   001.6'4'023   74-4148
ISBN 0-8104-5916-7
ISBN 0-8104-5915-9 (pbk.)

1	2	3	4	5	6	7	8	9	PRINTING
74	75	76	77	78	79	80	81	82	YEAR

Preface

The electronic digital computer has perhaps had more effect on people around the world than any other device invented by twentieth-century man. Its future seems to be relatively unlimited. Our lives are being influenced by these machines, and in many cases are actually dependent on them.

A decade ago, only a handful of teachers, scientists, engineers, mathematicians, and businessmen really understood the computer and its application to contemporary problems. Today, regardless of one's role in society, a minimum knowledge of computers is essential for everyone. The purpose of this book is to show the almost unbelievably wide range of computer applications. Medicine, law, engineering, transportation, business, and education are only a few of the fields in which the computer has become a vital tool.

How does the computer really affect people and society? What is its future? Can it be used to help the artist, the sports announcer, the housewife? What is computer dating? This book provides the answers to hundreds of such up-to-the-minute questions. It can be used as a textbook in introductory courses in computer applications since it requires no previous knowledge about the subject. It can also be used for supplementary reading assignments to broaden the content of programming or computer appreciation courses in community colleges and universities.

An attempt has been made to keep the computer jargon and technical terms to a minimum. This book is intended to be readable, and many cartoons and illustrations supplement the text. For those completely unfamiliar with the field, an introductory chapter briefly describes computers, and a glossary of computer terms closes the book. Each chapter discusses a different application area. Chapters may be read in any order or omitted altogether without causing any difficulties for the reader. Supplemental readings conclude each chapter.

I would like to express my sincere appreciation to innumerable computer manufacturers, educational institutions, government agencies, and businesses for providing the photographs and illustrations used in this book, and a special note of thanks to my wife for her help in typing the manuscript.

This book is dedicated to the kids of the present generation, especially mine — Michael, Laura, Steven, Sherrie, Susan, and Sandra. Tens of thousands of them, perhaps hundreds of thousands, will one day use computers. I'm very curious to see what they will accomplish with them!

DONALD D. SPENCER

Computer in Society — 18

Computer and the future
166

Contents

COMPUTERS
IN SOCIETY

1

The Story of Computers

The Importance of Computers

Many forces acting singly and in concert have set the world into turbulent motion. The computer, a relatively new invention, deserves credit for some of the ferment. It may do more to modify the shape and destiny of our world than did the invention of the wheel, the printing press, the telephone, the automobile, or electric power. No life will be left untouched by the pace of the technological revolution to which it is a principal contributor. It would be unrealistic to assume that most of our institutions will remain unaltered in a society so committed to the unending change that this revolution promotes.

The computer is now becoming available to a large segment of the population and is beginning to have an impact on our everyday life. It is reshaping century-old ways of doing things. This machine, man's most remarkable invention, is invading every nook and cranny of society, opening up vast new possibilities by its extraordinary feats of rapid manipulation. It has made it possible to multiply by many millions of times the capabilities of the human mind. In short, it is becoming so essential a tool, with so much potential for changing our lives and our world, that it is essential that everyone know something about it.

Computers have radically altered the world of business. They have opened up new horizons to the fields of science and medicine, improved the efficiency of government, and changed the techniques of education. They have affected military strategy, increased human productivity, made many products less expensive, and lowered the barriers to knowledge.

Computers route long-distance telephone calls, set newspaper type, help design automobiles, navigate ships, mix cakes, prepare weather forecasts, check income tax returns, direct city traffic, diagnose patients, compose music, play chess, streamline bank operations, schedule classes, grade test papers, and reserve seats on an airplane.

Computers can store every variety of information recorded by man and almost instantly recall it for use. They can calculate tens of millions of times faster than the brain and solve in seconds many problems that would take batteries of experts years to complete. No one should have to spend long hours adding endless columns of numbers, entering accounts in ledgers, keeping inventory records, making out bills or checks. But this is all good and proper work for a computer. Beyond such mundane chores, of course, the computer does vital jobs that could never be done fast enough by unaided human minds. If the computer had not been developed, for example, American astronauts would have been unable to venture to the moon.

Computers have given science and technology the greatest tool ever developed for turning the forces of nature to human use. The reason is simple. The computer is more than a prodigy of information and analysis. It also never forgets what it has acquired. In time, it will even respond to oral command and report in both written and spoken English.

Through space satellites and data communications links, all fields of information will some day be instantly available from computer centers around the globe and automatically translated into the language of the user. Eventually, the computer will program many of its own activities and even help to design and build better computers.

Computers in Use

Computer technology has improved at a tremendously fast pace during the past 20 years. During the past decade alone computer equipment has become 10 times smaller, 100 times faster, and 1000 times less expensive to operate. When computers were originally developed, many thought that only a few large businesses could use them; they were seen as too powerful, costly, and complicated for most concerns. Furthermore, most people were skeptical of their abilities or feared their threat to the comfortable status quo.

Most computers of the 1940's were used for scientific computations and were located at government or large university facilities. During the 1950's big business began experimentation and research to determine if computers could handle its routine work. Management was looking for an automated administrative function to produce quicker and better reports, replace clerical employees, perform during employment shortages, and manage a mounting surge of paperwork handling.

In the 1960's computers began to be used in applications not even envisioned in the 1950's. The 1970's are likely to be years when the computer will directly affect our way of living at everv turn. It may eventually become as much a part of home life as the family automobile or television set, and as much a part of school life as the classroom projector.

In 1950 there were only 15 computers in the United States, and a year later, less than 100. The 1,000 mark was passed five years later, in 1956. By 1961, there were over 10,000 computers in the world, 95 percent of them in the United States. By 1966 there were over 40,000. By mid 1972 there were about

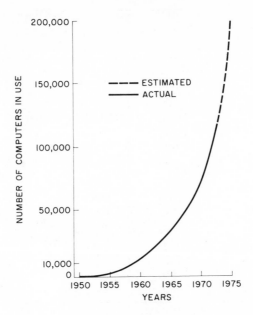

Number of computers in use.

100,000 being used in the United States alone, in all kinds of businesses, educational institutions, and scientific and government organizations (according to the Diebold computer census). It is estimated that over 200,000 computers will be in use by 1975, and by 1980 perhaps 350,000. The computer industry is already the twelfth largest industry in the United States and growing faster than many of those leading the list.

Computer users around the globe today are operating about 25 billion dollars worth of equipment. The historical growth rate of 15 to 20 percent a year is expected to continue into the next decade. By 1980 the value of computing equipment may be around 75 billion dollars.

A 1972 estimate of the worldwide use of computers is shown in the following table. These numbers were compiled from hundreds of source documents. In some cases the estimate has been extrapolated to represent the number of installations.

Country	Number of installations	Country	Number of installations
United States	100,000	West Germany	9,000
Japan	15,000	U.S.S.R.	7,000
France	9,000	Great Britain	5,000

Country	Number of installations	Country	Number of installations
Italy	4,500	Finland	250
Canada	4,500	Israel	250
The Netherlands	1,200	Norway	207
Australia	1,000	Arab Countries	164
Belgium	1,000	Hungary	120
Brazil	900	Yugoslavia	116
Spain	800	Philippines	106
Sweden	800	China	100
Mexico	500	India	100
Argentina	460	Greece	60
Austria	440	Rumania	50
Denmark	400	Lebanon	40
Czechoslovakia	300	Singapore	40
Poland	300	Taiwan	40
Venezuela	300	Thailand	31

Computer costs range from several million dollars a system to a few thousand dollars. Units are now available that cost less than $3,000. By 1975 a small computer should go for around $1,000.

What Computers Cannot Do

Of all myths about computers, perhaps the most widespread and in the long run the most dangerous is the one that goes: *computers think for you.* A computer can no more think for you than can a screwdriver or the automobile you drive. Indeed, the actions of a dog in reacting to external influences more closely resemble those of a man than those of a computer, but who would expect his dog to *think* for him?

Although the computer is extremely fast, it is absolutely incapable of doing anything but carrying out the instructions written for it and placed into it by human beings. It has no more intelligence than a hammer and is totally useless without human beings directing its operations.

Can a computer invent its own problems? No, computers do not think and therefore they cannot create their own problems. They can never reproduce or replace the human thinking process. Computers can manipulate and combine items of *data,* but they cannot, beyond the strict limits of their instructions (called *programs*), infer any meaning or *information* from this result. Human beings make such inferences with great facility, both consciously and unconsciously.

A computer is instructed (via a computer program) to perform a series of logic and arithmetic operations by a human being who knows the *language* of the computer. The human being, then, is the person who commands the computer. The computer is his electronic slave, just as the huge elephant working in a tropical forest is the slave of his mahout. The man does the thinking; the computer or the elephant does the work.

The computer is a willing slave and will perform whatever it is instructed to do. However, it will produce a million incorrect answers just as fast as a million correct ones. Human beings must thus exercise great care in preparing its instructions. These must be absolutely unambiguous, precise and complete to the last detail. Otherwise the computer may produce unexpected answers. Answers of this sort are often mislabeled "creative answers" as if the computer had actually engaged in "creative thought" simply because it provided information that was previously unknown to the user. All the computer has actually done is to carry out the instructions that were specified beforehand. The reason the results were a surprise is probably that there were so many calculations to be made or facts to be analyzed that no one could estimate offhand what the outcome would be.

Certain human acts are indispensable to the functioning of computers. The human being must first conceive the need for the computer's work, he must then prepare the instructions for this work, and he must finally start the process. It will thus be a long time, if ever, before computers pose a supreme challenge to man. For all his shortcomings, man is uniquely capable of responding to unforeseeable contingencies for which there is neither precedent nor experience. Instinct, intuition, inspiration have raised man to his highest peaks, and the computer will never attain comparable levels. The following comment was made by President John F. Kennedy, May 21, 1963, when he welcomed astronaut Gordon Cooper to Washington after the officer took over control of his space capsule to achieve a safe splash-down in the Pacific:

" ... However extraordinary computers may be ... man is still the most extraordinary computer of all."

Can a computer make value judgments about things, that is, can it answer such questions as "Is it beautiful?" "Does it have a fragrant smell?" "Is it ethical?" The problems posed by such questions are so difficult to handle with a computer that those who try must almost always be rewarded with unimaginative, fragmentary results. Here then is another of man's irreplaceable roles—the use of wisdom and judgment. A computer may help with such problems only by retrieving or processing any relevant data; the human being is then left to his common sense and experience to make the decisions.

Human beings (some of them) have imaginations and therefore the ability to create the mental image of something new. Attempts have been made by various experimenters to lead computers into elementary forms of creativity. Computers have been programmed to write music, draw pictures, write stories and plays, compose poetry, and design patterns. So far the results have been rather limited. A computer, having no imagination of its own, is finally dependent on man for the ability to create.

Types of Computers

When someone asks, "What is a computer?," we have to reply, "What kind of computer do you mean?" The reason for this is that there are two basic types of computers: the *analog* and the *digital*.

Analog computers solve problems by measuring such *continuously* occurring variable physical conditions as pressure, voltage, temperature, speed, or position and translating these measurements into a continuous, meaningful output form. Several simple examples of analog devices are the slide rule, automobile speedometer, thermostat, hourglass, and thermometer.

The *digital computer*—the most versatile machine of the electronic computer family—performs calculations by counting, by its nature a discrete, *noncontinuous* operation. The digital computer can represent information only as discrete numbers and works on data mathematically rather than physically. There are two types: the *special-purpose computer*, which is designed for only one application, and the *general-purpose computer*, which may be used in many different applications. (Most general-purpose computers are of the *stored-program* type, that is, they store their instructions in their internal memory.)

The desk calculator and abacus are simple examples of digital devices. Others are telephone dials, ticker tapes, punched cards, and light-bulb-display time-and-temperature signs.

How the Computer Works

Although computers differ widely in size, cost, and capabilities, they are all organized similarly and include five functional units. The *storage unit* is used to hold data, program instructions, and intermediate and final results of calculations. The *arithmetic unit* performs the common arithmetic operations: addition, subtraction, multiplication, division, and comparison. The *input* and *output* units provide for communications with external equipment such as card readers, high-speed printers, magnetic-tape units, display devices, typewriters, and many other similar devices. All internal functions of the computer are performed under the "watchful eye" of the *control unit*, which directs the operations as specified by a computer program.

The control unit, storage unit, and arithmetic unit make up what is usually called the *central processing unit* (CPU) of the computer.

The *computer program* is not part of the digital computer hardware described above, but it is the prime source of control of the computer's operations. The program is put in the computer's storage unit, and the computer follows whatever sequence is specified by the program instructions.

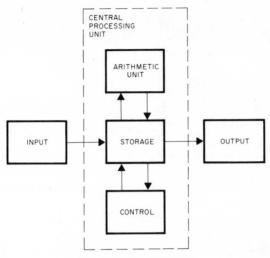

Schematic of a computer.

To illustrate the functions of a computer we can compare its operations with those of a human operator solving a problem with an adding machine. The human operator takes his problem from his input basket, computes the totals and other calculations required, and places the piece of paper from the adding machine (which contains the results) in his outgoing basket. The computer would solve the same problem using its functional counterparts by reading into storage the data to be worked on, performing the calculations, and outputting the results. The computer must, of course, have a computer program in its storage that can guide the entire operation, as the human operator did in the manual case. The comparison of the computer and the human being is summarized in the following table:

Computer	Human being
Input Equipment	Input Basket
Arithmetic Unit	Adding Machine
Storage	Adding Machine Paper
Control Unit (activated by the program)	Human Operator
Output Equipment	Output Basket

Elements of the Computer System

A *computer system* consists of a number of individual components, each of which has its own function. The system consists of units to prepare input information, equipment to send information to the computer, the computer itself, auxiliary storage units, and equipment to accept information from the

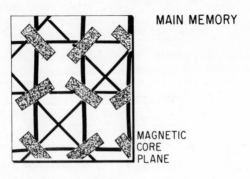

MAIN MEMORY

MAGNETIC
CORE
PLANE

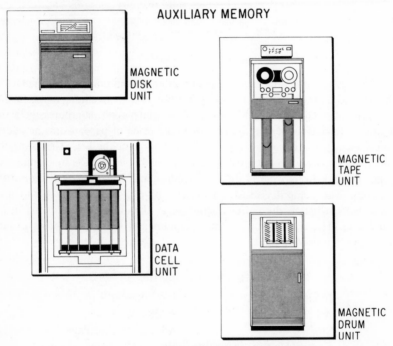

AUXILIARY MEMORY

MAGNETIC
DISK
UNIT

MAGNETIC
TAPE
UNIT

DATA
CELL
UNIT

MAGNETIC
DRUM
UNIT

Storage devices.

computer. Complementing the *hardware* of many systems is a *software* system that includes a control program and other programs that aid the user in preparing computer programs.

Input information is usually prepared by card keypunches or paper tape-punching units. These units are sometimes called *data preparation units* and are never directly connected to the computer.

Input and *output devices* are connected to the computer and their function is to read information into and out of the storage unit. Common input devices are card readers, paper-tape readers, magnetic-ink character readers, optical scanners, and typewriters. Problem results are often recorded on high-speed printers, typewriters, display units, plotters, paper-tape punches, and card punches. These units are called output devices.

The capability of a computer to indefinitely store and retrieve information is one of its fundamental and most essential facilities. This facility is called its *memory*. What does the word "memory" actually mean? When a human being remembers something, he recalls it instantaneously from a storage area within his brain. In many respects, although this is still a strongly disputed point, the storage devices of a computer are similar to the storage area of a human brain. Instructions and data facts are stored in the computer's memory where they may be rapidly recalled whenever needed.

There are two classifications of computer memory: *internal* and *auxiliary*. *Internal memory* is used to store instructions and data during processing. *Auxiliary memory* is used to supplement the internal memory.

The internal memory of most modern-day computers consists of many thousands of small *magnetic cores*. A core looks like a little doughnut and is made of a metallic material (such as iron oxide) that is easily magnetized. The cores are strung like beads on insulated wires. When a current of sufficient strength is passed through a wire, the cores attached to it are magnetized in the direction of the current's flow. If the direction of the current flow is reversed, the magnetic state of the core is also reversed. This property makes it possible to represent two different states, the first by magnetizing the core in one direction and the second by magnetizing it in the other direction. Since these two states can be identified as the two binary numbers 1 and 0, the computer is enabled to perform all its calculations by binary arithmetic.

A typical-size magnetic-core memory of a medium-size computer will include over a million cores.

Auxiliary memories are used to supplement the computer's internal memory and ordinarily store considerably more information. Common devices used for auxiliary memory are magnetic drums, magnetic discs, magnetic cards, magnetic tapes, and large banks of magnetic cores.

Computer Instructions and Programming

Now that we have looked at the hardware of a computer system, let's look into the software. *Software* is a general term that applies to everything other than *hardware* that is used in a computer system. One usually thinks of software as being the instructions that direct the operation of a computer, plus the various paper documents detailing the system.

A *computer program* is a set of instructions that tell the computer how to perform some specific calculation or operation. It is via the program that one communicates a problem to the computer. Each instruction in the program is a direction to the computer to perform some simple operation, such as adding two

A computer system consisting of a Univac 9400 computer (top right), six magnetic tape units (at left), three magnetic disk units (center), a typewriter console, a printer (top left), and a card reader and punch (bottom). (*Courtesy,* Univac Div., Sperry Rand Corp.)

numbers or printing a line of results. The computer will follow the sequence of instructions in a program without deviating and is thus able to solve problems without human intervention.

A computer program may be written in one of several available programming languages. One such language is *machine language,* which is written in binary, octal, or hexadecimal numbers. Since this language is very difficult to work with, it is seldom used.

A language on the same level as machine language, but one that uses symbolic codes rather than numbers, is called *assembly language.* This language is simpler for a user, since easy-to-use symbols are employed to represent computer instructions, storage locations, etc. An assembly language program is translated into machine language by an *assembler* prior to being run on the computer. The assembler is, in itself, another program whose sole function is to translate a program written in assembly language into the only language that the computer itself understands: machine language.

Another programming language that is very easy to use is called *procedure-oriented* or *compiler language.* This is a high-level language that resembles the English language. A command in this language will take the place of many machine-language or assembly-language instructions. Compiler languages are very popular, primarily because they simplify the software development task. Since they do not require the user to have a detailed knowledge of the computer, he can concentrate more deeply on steps more closely related to the problem he is coding.

Before a program written in a compiler language can be run on a computer, however, it must be compiled. This process consists of translating the program into machine language. The translator for this process is called a *compiler.*

Six popular compiler languages are: (1) FORTRAN (FORmula TRANslation), a language that is primarily used for solving engineering and mathematical problems; (2) COBOL (COmmon Business Oriented Language), a language intended for business-type applications; (3) PI/1, a general language used for solving problems of various natures; (4) BASIC (Beginner's All-purpose Symbolic Instruction Code), an easy-to-learn language used with most time-sharing and minicomputer systems; (5) RPG (Report Program Generator), a language used to produce common business reports; and (6) ALGOL (ALGOrithmic Language), a mathematical-type language.

Let us use the problem, $y = x^2 + b - 37$, to illustrate the complexity of each of the three languages being discussed. A set of instructions in the English language to perform this computation might be as follows:

1. Place x in a working register* of the computer
2. Multiply the register by x
3. Add b to the register
4. Subtract 37 from the register
5. Store the register in a storage position identified by y

In machine language the instructions to accomplish the computation might be as follows:

Binary		*Octal*	
001000	100000000	10	400
001010	100000000	12	400
011110	110011000	36	630
011111	000011111	37	037
100001	110000000	41	600

In assembly language it might be as follows:

CLA	X
MUL	X
ADD	B
SUB	37
STR	Y

*A working register is a hardware device for storing one unit of data that is to be manipulated.

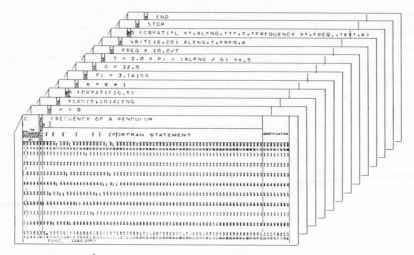

A computer program (written in the Fortran language) represented on punched cards.

And in compiler language, it might be as follows:

$$LET \; Y = X**2 + B - 37$$

Even though these instructions represent a solution to a very simple calculation, they point out that high-level compiler language instructions are much easier to read and work with than are low-level assembly or machine language instructions.

Can Computers Make Mistakes?

Human beings can make mistakes in arithmetic, adding 24 and 7 to get 32, putting a decimal point in the wrong place, multiplying 326 by 4 to get 1204. They write and copy numbers incorrectly. They make judgment mistakes, filing mistakes, identification mistakes, all kinds of mistakes. These are strictly human mistakes and are *not* the kind that a computer makes.

A computer will perform *exactly* the job that it is instructed to do. However, there may be inherent errors in the computer instructions that will make the computer *appear* to make the kind of mistakes listed above. Defects in computer instructions, needless to say, are the fault of the person who prepared them, not of the computer.

Human mistakes have resulted in fouling up billing procedures, payrolls, traffic routing, purchase orders, production orders, and countless other procedures. For example, the computer might be given an order for 50 pairs of shoes, and because of a defect in the program, it might cause a purchase order to be printed for 50 dozen pair, not being capable of recognizing this as a mistake.

Most mistakes of this type can be avoided by careful preparation of computer instructions (including instructions containing "plausibility ranges" for valid transactions) or by correcting the mistake when it is first detected.

There is another type of human mistake that is called GIGO by computer users. GIGO means *garbage in–garbage out* and is a way of saying that if there is an error in the data fed into a computer, or if that data is incomplete or in the wrong sequence of presentation, then the computer will *process* it as instructed, all right, but the resulting output—whether a customer bill, a paycheck, or an airline seat reservation—cannot be right.

So much for *human mistakes.* Let us now look at some computer "mistakes," called *computer malfunctions.* Computers are susceptible to extreme environmental conditions such as temperature, humidity, polluted or salt air, and dust. Designers attempt to guard against such conditions, but computers can still malfunction when operating under them. Many computers built for military use—such as aboard a ship, in a tank, spacecraft, airplane or missile—are designed with their specific environments in mind.

A computer can also malfunction when some foreign electric disturbance takes place that affects the electric pulses through all its parts. A few pulses here and there can cause a large amount of trouble that may not be detected immediately.

Data transmission *errors* may occur during thunderstorms or solar storms. Such errors cause the data being transmitted to or from a computer to be distorted, resulting in incorrect printouts or calculations. Magnetically stored data are vulnerable also. If a strong magnetic disturbance takes place, it may erase or alter data stored on a *medium* in the form of magnetic bits. Computational errors can also occur in the computer whenever numbers being manipulated become too large or too small.

Computer Numbering Systems

The circuitry of a computer consists of elements that may physically be on or off, closed or open, and the like, and the storage of a computer is composed of magnetic cores that can be magnetized in a clockwise or counterclockwise direction. These bistable elements provide for only two conditions, and this is the reason computers use a *binary* numbering system. (Elements with more than two stable states exist, but they are currently more expensive and less reliable than bistable devices.)

The binary system is composed of only two digits: 1 and 0. A binary 1 can represent a magnetic core's being magnetized in one direction or a circuit's being open. Likewise, a 0 can represent a magnetic core's being magnetized in the opposite direction or a circuit's being closed.

The binary system is the simplest of all numbering systems. It has a base, or radix, of 2, which means that each position in a binary number is represented by a value of some power of 2. For example, the decimal number 37 is represented as 100101 in the binary numbering system and may be interpreted as follows: $1 \times 2^5 + 0 \times 2^4 + 0 \times 2^3 + 1 \times 2^2 + 0 \times 2^1 + 1 \times 2^0$, which equals $32 + 0 + 0 + 4 + 0 + 1 = 37$.

As binary numbers become large, they become extremely clumsy for people to work with. It is for this reason that computer users, if not the computers themselves, use other numbering systems to represent binary numbers. The *octal* and *hexadecimal numbering systems* quite often serve this purpose. In order to illustrate the value of these systems, consider the binary number, 101 111 001 011 011 001 110 101, which may be represented in octal as 57133165 and in hexadecimal as BCB675. It should be obvious that working with an 8-digit octal or a 6-digit hexadecimal number is much simpler than with a binary number that contains 24 digits.

A Brief History

Up to now we have talked about the importance of computers, and the hardware and software aspects of computer systems. Let us now look at how it all started.

Aside from the ten fingers, tally sticks, and pebble counting, the earliest known computing device is the *abacus*. This ancient Chinese invention is still one of the most widely used calculators throughout the world. It can be used for adding, subtracting, multiplying, dividing, and taking square roots. The Japanese built a similar device and called it a *soroban.*

Another significant computational device came in 1614, when John Napier invented and published a table of *logarithms*. In 1617 he proceeded to devise a computing system called *Napier's bones*. These were simply a set of numbering rods to simplify multiplication, division, and extraction of roots. Napier's logarithms were used in 1630 by William Oughtred, who inscribed logarithmic scales on ivory rods and thus invented the *slide rule.*

In 1642, the nineteen-year-old Frenchman Blaise Pascal, irritated with the task of adding long columns of figures for his tax-collector father, invented the *first mechanical calculating machine.* The most important feature of this machine was the built-in, automatic means for carrying. Later in the same century (1671), the German mathematician Leibniz developed a machine that could do multiplication by rapidly repeated addition.

One of the most-used forms of input in a modern computing system is the *punched card.* The card concept is quite old; a similar medium was used in French fabric looms of the eighteenth century—the so-called Jacquard loom. Herman Hollerith, an employee of the U.S. Bureau of Census, applied the punched-hole principle to cards and had them sorted mechanically for the 1890 census. Census information was hand-punched on the cards, each card containing facts about one person: age, sex, and the like. Hollerith's punched cards and tabulator enabled the Census Bureau to complete the 1890 census in two years, one-third of the time that was required to take the 1880 census, yet the U.S. population had risen from 50,262,000 to 63,056,000.

Charles Babbage, early in the nineteenth century, developed the fore-runner of today's automatic digital computer. He designed two machines: the *Difference Engine* and the *Analytical Engine*. These machines were never built, because of various engineering problems of that era. Babbage was a man before his time; his analytical engine had a punched-card input, it had storage for 50,000 decimal digits, it had an arithmetic unit, it had a control unit, and it presented output documents that were either printed forms or punched cards. This machine contained all the basic parts of a modern-day computer, and it was designed in 1833.

In 1944, more than a hundred years after Babbage developed the analytical engine, Dr. Howard Aiken, with assistance from IBM engineers and Harvard graduate students, completed the *Automatic Sequence Controlled Calculator* (ASCC), commonly known as the Mark I. The principle of operation was mechanical, but relays were used. Although this machine was a slow calculator, it has a permanent place in the history of calculating machines: It was the *first automatic calculating machine* ever built.

The *first electronic automatic computer* to be built was the *Electric Numerical Integrator and Computer* (ENIAC). It was the first computer to make use of electronic circuits. The ENIAC was designed by J. Presper Eckert and John W. Mauchly and built by coworkers at the Moore School of Electrical Engineering, University of Pennsylvania, in 1946. This computer could perform an addition in 200 microseconds (a microsecond is a millionth of a second) and a ten-digit multiplication in 2.8 milliseconds (a millisecond is a thousandth of a second). It contained 19,000 vacuum tubes, weighed about 30 tons, and filled an area of more than 1,500 square feet. The ENIAC may now be found in the Smithsonian Institution in Washington, D.C.

The *Electronic Discrete Variable Automatic Computer* (EDVAC) was also built at the Moore School of Electrical Engineering, this one in 1949. Used to compute ballistic and weapon-systems evaluation problems, it cost around half a million dollars and could add two numbers in 864 microseconds.

The world's first commercial data-processing computer went into operation in March 1951. It was installed at the U.S. Bureau of the Census and was called *Univac I*. The first Univac I computer is also now located in the Smithsonian Institution. It was retired there in 1963 after twelve and one-half years of operation and 73,000 hours of use.

Early IBM computers were the IBM 650 and IBM 704. In 1964, IBM introduced the System/360 computers. To date, more 360 computers have been made than the total number of computers made by other manufacturers.

All the early computers had used *vacuum tubes* as basic components of internal circuits. As a result, the machines were huge, needed considerable power to run, and had to be repaired every few hours. These machines belonged to what is called the *first generation* of computers.

(A)   (B)   (C)

Comparison of circuitry devices used in computers: (a) Vacuum tube, (b) transistor, and (c) integrated circuit. (*Courtesy,* IBM corp.)

Research soon led to the development of computers that used *transistors* instead of vacuum tubes. These machines, which were called *second generation* computers, were more reliable, consumed less power, were smaller, produced less heat, and had much more storage capacity. The use of transistors also increased their processing speed.

The next generation of computers, introduced when IBM announced the System/360 in 1964, used *microminiature circuits*, usually called *integrated circuits*. These *third generation* machines allow faster execution of instructions, are more reliable, and have large-capacity storage facilities. Most third generation computer systems are designed to handle both business and scientific data processing with equal ease. Many earlier machines were directed toward processing either business or scientific applications, but not both.

With the third generation computer came a new term for speed: *nanosecond*. A nanosecond is one billionth (1/1,000,000,000) of a second. Some of the internal processing of data within these machines is performed at nanosecond speed. Other slower operations are performed in microseconds and milliseconds.

The fourth generation of computers will probably appear during the late 1970's and will use very compact circuitry, thus further increasing the computational speed and reducing the cost of computers.

Recommended Reading

Benice, D.D., *Introduction to Computers and Data Processing,* Prentice-Hall, 1970.

Brown, J. A., *Computers and Automation,* Arco, 1968.

Clark, F. J., *Information Processing,* Goodyear, 1970.

Davis, G. B., *An Introduction to Electronic Computers,* 2nd ed. McGraw-Hill, 1971.

Gerald, C. F., *Computers and the Art of Computation,* Addison-Wesley, 1972, Chap. 1.

Price, W. T., *Introduction to Data Processing,* Rinehart Press, 1972.

Saxon, J. A. and Steyer, W. W., *Basic Principles of Data Processing,* Prentice-Hall, 1970.

Spencer, D. D., *Everything You Wanted to Know About Computers,* Hayden, 1974.

Spencer, D. D., *Introduction to Information Processing,* Charles E. Merrill, 1974.

Scientific American, Computers and Computation, W. H. Freeman and Co., 1971, Chap. 11.

Tatham, L., *Computers in Everyday Life,* Pelham Books (London), 1970, Chap. 7.

Trask, M., *The Story of Cybernetics,* Dutton, 1971.

2

The Computer in Society

Impact of the Computer

The electronic computer, not yet thirty years old, has come of age, progressing from scientific curiosity to essential part of civilization in a remarkably short time. In many respects, computers have erased time, altered the ordinary relationships that affect our lives and our organizations, and accelerated the rate of change to the point that someone once entitled a speech, "The Effect of Computers on Progress, or, By the Time You've Said It, It's Happened!" As an indication of the degree of assimilation of computers into our society, just imagine what would happen if they were suddenly withdrawn from service. Airline travel would be chaotically disrupted, industrial systems would grind to a halt, banks would bulge with unprocessed paper, and much in our lives that we now take for granted suddenly would be no more.

After each major technological development, it has possibly been truthful to say, "The world will never again be the same." These products of technology have radically altered the pattern of our private and business lives. They have certainly increased our mobility, eliminated tedious physical labor, provided convenient means of communication. However, each of these products has also plagued society with ills, problems, and frustrations.

Take as only one example the impact of the automobile. The automobile has totally changed this nation—its living standards, its housing patterns, its work and recreation habits, and, above all, its transportation. It now causes over 20 deaths per 100,000 population per year and at its outset created a moral problem of sorts by providing unmarried young people with a privacy they had never before enjoyed.

Will the computer change society more radically than the automobile? There are many strong indications that it will do so in the future. If, for example, developments in computers and communications should enable many people to work and learn at home, there might be no need for huge offices and crowded schools. The implications for society of such a change are enormous.

Does the computer pose a threat or offer support to "life, liberty, and the pursuit of happiness"? Looking to the past, few would disagree that the net impact of technological developments has been favorable. It is unfortunate to have to turn to the past and scan the present for indications of the future but that is all the evidence we have. This does not mean that the future will be like the past and present. It never has been. It only means that extension of past trends tempered by judgments of the impact of impending developments is the scientific substitute for the spirit of prophecy.

Technology is a tool neutral between good and evil. We have used it for both, and the greater the potential for good, of course, the greater the potential for evil. We have in our hands untested technologies of tremendous power. It is too early to tell whether they will be used to build or destroy. The computer's potential, of course, is not as extreme in either direction, but many people have raised questions concerning its value to society.

Although early computer developments were conducted in Great Britain and Germany, the computer is essentially an American invention. Today the United States uses more computers than the rest of the world combined. The United States, however, is not the only country that manufactures computers. Computer makers may be found in Japan, Germany, France, The U.S.S.R., Great Britain, Italy, The Netherlands, Israel, Norway, Sweden, Poland, and several other countries. Since the United States leads the world in computer usage, it also has a head start in some of the social problems resulting from their use. Other nations (especially Japan, West Germany, Australia, France and Great Britain), however, are also beginning to suffer from some of the problem symptoms.

Computer Attitudes

People often ask questions such as the following: Are computers more clever than people? Do they have feelings of love and hate? Can they think for themselves? Can they outwit humans? Can they replace people at performing everyday jobs? Will they run the world and make slaves of human beings?

Everyone has heard at least something about computers on television, at the movies, in books, newspapers, or magazines. Probably most of the articles and pictures have been rather sensational—"Computer Makes a Mistake and Overpays XYZ Company Employees by $2,000,000," "Computer Causes the African Bulldogs To Lose Football Championship," "Computer Causes Rocket To Go Off Target." Cartoonists delight in giving computers robot-like stature and minds of their own that like to play tricks on ordinary mortals. Names for computers have included human analogies like *electronic brain* or *mechanical brain.*

It is no wonder that the general public is often confused about computers. They don't know that many of the news items are utter nonsense or in error because of poor facts or poor understanding on the part of a journalist. Of

BUSINESS AUTOMATION

"Did it have any enemies?"

course, the press, TV, and radio have long been accustomed to stressing the odd or exciting elements in their news in order to capture the attention of their audiences. Only sensational stories receive widespread publicity. Consequently, much of the public blames computers (rather than the people using them) for problems that arise in data processing applications. Can you imagine blaming an automobile when an accident occurred? Or a hammer because it hit you on the thumb?

Over the past few years a number of computer centers have been demolished by misguided individuals, including even university students. Some people take delight in folding, stapling, and mutilating punched cards (utility bills, magazine subscription cards, school registration cards, and so forth) simply because they know that it will disrupt their normal computer processing. A man in London, England went so far as to place a punched card on a drawing board and carefully cut out three or four extra holes with a razor blade in order to change the information on the card and so confound the computer altogether.

Automation and Employment

Automation is the process of replacing human work with work done by a machine or system designed to perform a specific combination of actions automatically or repeatedly. For example, a machine used in the automotive industry transforms rough metal castings and other components into finished auto engines. The computer is another machine that can perform jobs automatically. Since many of these jobs have been or are still classified as human occupations, the computer poses a threat to numerous workers and their jobs.

Author L. Frank Baum shared the turn-of-century optimism about machines as a positive force. An admired (if not beloved) character in his famous Oz series was Tik-tok, the clockwork copper man who "was sure to do exactly what he was wound up to do, at all times and in all circumstances." That a machine "would only do the special kind of thing it had been calculated to do" was regarded as no defect by philosopher Charles S. Peirce, who observed: "We do not want it to do its own business, but ours."

It is pointless to argue whether automation destroys or creates employment. Its purpose is to reduce the costs of production or to perform tasks that could not otherwise be done. In either case, it is a substitute as well as a supplement for human labor. We might argue, as some do, that since "society" benefits from automation, "society" should provide retraining and interim support for those who are displaced by automation.

Actually, in many instances automation displaces no one. (It has been estimated that approximately one-half of the U.S. labor force would be required to staff current telephone switchboards if automatic switching and other devices had not been installed in the past.) If over the years the mechanization of physical tasks has displaced millions of people, however, most of them have been able to make the adjustment with discomfort but without great pain. The tragedies were of two types: 1) Displacements that occurred in periods of inadequate demand when alternative job opportunities were not being created rapidly enough, and 2) displacements that affected people (for example, coal miners and cotton pickers) who were unprepared and unable to compete in other fields.

Few people have been displaced by computerization. If and when computer displacement occurs, it will likely be less painful in that its impact will be primarily on managerial, clerical, and skilled workers who are better prepared for adapting themselves to other jobs. Often whenever an employee's job is to be replaced by a computerized system, he is retrained to work in some other area rather than laid off. The installation of a computer, moreover, always entails the creation of new jobs. People are required to maintain, operate, and program the computer system. Displaced personnel may very well find new positions as keypunchers, computer operators, programmers, and so forth.

Privacy and Data Banks

Man has a natural aversion to becoming a statistic, a mere figure to be mulled over, like the highway death count on a July 4th weekend. Yet, for all its tremendous benefits, computerization may be doing just that: threatening the one sanctity man has left—his right to privacy.

Information concerning an individual can be represented on a tiny portion of a reel of magnetic tape. The fact that such information about ourselves (the 1's and 0's of our lives) can be stored in a computerized system need not be wholly distasteful. The realization, however, that in much less than a second an entire lifetime can be translated for anyone clever enough to gain access to such a system most certainly *is*.

Although privacy is not mentioned by name in the Constitution, the Bill of Rights contains guarantees against all methods to invade privacy that were prevalent in the eighteenth century. A man cannot be compelled to give up his home to quarter troops; a man cannot be forced to give testimony against himself. Perhaps most important are the words of the Fourth Amendment:

> "The right of the people to be secure in their persons, houses, papers, and effects, against unreasonable searches and seizures, shall not be violated. . . ."

Congressman Cornelius E. Gallagher (Democrat, New Jersey), a strong critic of the computer's "invasion of privacy," has remarked, "The computer can be used to elevate man—as it has delivered him to the moon—or it can be used to enslave him."

One can easily pose many vital questions concerning the use of files of personal data. For example, how can society maintain the relevance of *due process of law* when reels of tape containing the intimate personal details of millions of lives can be instantly transferred from a computer in one jurisdiction to a computer in another? How can a man face his accuser when his records are submerged in an inaccessible data bank that he scarcely knows exists, much less has the technical expertise to question? If a national data bank is formed, who will control the data?

It is now entirely feasible for a government or a private agency to construct files of personal information for interrogation by remote computer consoles. Data about an individual obtained from different sources can be matched and used without the person's knowledge by anybody with access to the system. The increasing use of the Social Security Number as a unique identifier for each person makes this data matching possible. What safeguards do we need against the establishment of such information banks, against the accuracy of their data input and the potential use of their data? Are special congressional bills required to protect the rights of the individual against the invasion of his privacy by such banks? Many people think they are.

Their fears are not wholly misplaced. All of us leave a trail of records behind us as we go through life, but they are widely dispersed and inaccessible in composite. The day of judgment when all our secret acts are to be revealed is remote enough to cause no discomfort. Just how would we like it to occur here and now? Consider the hypothetical "Daily Information Sheet" on Robert Smith shown on pages 24–25. It should illustrate the need for the public's concern very well indeed.

The Federal State of Hesse in West Germany has established a government data bank that will contain about seventy items of personal information on each Hesse citizen. Simultaneously, the Hesse Parliament has enacted legislation to prevent unauthorized or harmful use of the data. Safeguards include the appointment of a Data Protection Commissioner responsible to Parliament who will have ultimate responsibility for the system; procedures for investigation and possible compensation if a citizen feels he has been compromised through deliberate or accidental misuse of personal information; and a requirement that state and local legislative bodies be as informed about the stored data as the executive branch. One can only wonder just how long it will take before the system is misused. Americans can look upon their past adaptability as a reassurance of their ability to devise protections as they are needed, but it is only a reassurance, not a guarantee.

The Cashless-Checkless Society

The computer revolution is laying the groundwork for a future where a "universal credit card" geared to computerized data communications will be the only requirement for most financial transactions. This is the basis of the *cashless-checkless society* that government officials, bankers, and computer people foresee in the future. Their prediction is a response to the enormous challenge posed by banking's "paper tiger"—the huge and ever-increasing volume of checks generated by the nation's financial transactions.

Consider the following situation. In a hypothetical city, which we will call "Someplace, U.S.A.," a hypothetical lady, whom we will call Mrs. Cohoon, makes a trip to her shopping center where she purchases groceries for her family, shoes for her child, clothing for herself, and a case of beer for Mr. Cohoon. The only unusual aspect of this shopping trip, which is repeated daily by millions of housewives throughout the nation, is that Mrs. Cohoon paid for her purchases without money or check. Instead, she used a personal identification card. The data on the lady's purchases was transmitted to the shopping center's central communications office from which it was electronically relayed to the First National Utility of Someplace. Here, Mrs. Cohoon's purchases were debited from her account and the various stores where she had shopped received credit for their respective share of the total bill. All of these transactions were accomplished without an exchange of cash, checks, receipts, or any other paper.

Although such an episode has never yet occurred, it may very likely do so in the near future. The concept of the cashless-checkless economy has been with us for several years. However, recent developments in computer and communications facilities, along with a favorable environment in the banking community, have made it a more feasible possibility.

A cashless-checkless society exists today for some 3,000 checking account customers of Hempstead Bank in Syosset, a Long Island suburb of New York City. The customers at the bank are able to make purchases at 35 participating

---

CONFIDENTIAL
DAILY INFORMATION SHEET
NATIONAL DATA BANK
AUGUST 22, 1987

SUBJECT.   ROBERT SHIRLEY SMITH
            11036 COPLEY STREET
            ORLANDO, FLORIDA
            AGE 41
            MARRIED
            CHILDREN: JOHN, AGE 19; NANCY, AGE 14;
                       WILLIAM, AGE 12; JACK, AGE 6.
            PROFESSION: PLUMBER

PURCHASES. BREAKFAST   2.10
            GASOLINE   8.64
            NEWSPAPER   .10
            PHONE (867-2301)   .10
            PHONE (672-4467)   .10
            PHONE (772-3461)   .10
            PHONE (667-8841)   .10
            BANK (CASH WITHDRAWAL)   90.00
            LUNCH   6.20
            COCKTAILS   6.10
            PHONE (772-3461)   .10
            LINGERIE   35.70
            CHAMPAGNE   12.60
            NEWSPAPER   .10

**** COMPUTER ANALYSIS ****

LARGE BREAKFAST. USUALLY HAS ONLY COFFEE.

BOUGHT 8.64 DOLLARS GASOLINE. OWNS ECONOMY CAR. SO
FAR THIS WEEK HE HAS BOUGHT 21.40 DOLLARS WORTH OF
GAS. BOUGHT GASOLINE IN SANFORD, FLORIDA WHICH IS 32
MILES FROM HOME AND 37 MILES FROM WORK. BOUGHT GASO-
LINE AT 7:48. SAFE TO ASSUME HE WAS LATE TO WORK.

BOUGHT NEWSPAPER. HE ALWAYS READS THE PAPER WHEN HE GETS TO WORK.

PHONE NUMBER 867-2301 BELONGS TO EXPENSIVE MEN'S BARBER–SPECIALIZES IN HAIR STYLING AND BALD MEN.

PHONE NUMBER 672-4467 BELONGS TO HIS BOSS'S WIFE.

PHONE NUMBER 772-3461 BELONGS TO OLD GIRL FRIEND NAMED LULU ROCKET.

PHONE NUMBER 667-8841 BELONGS TO ATLAS TRAVEL AGENCY. MADE RESERVATIONS FOR MIAMI–SINGLE. FOURTH TRIP THIS YEAR TO MIAMI WITHOUT WIFE. WILL CHECK FILE TO SEE IF ANYONE ELSE HAS GONE TO MIAMI AT THE SAME TIME AND COMPARE TO HIS PHONE NUMBER CALLS.

WITHDREW 90.00 DOLLARS CASH. VERY UNUSUAL SINCE HE USUALLY USES HIS NATIONAL DATA CREDIT CARD FOR ALL PURCHASES AND TICKETS. CASH USUALLY USED ONLY FOR IL-LEGAL PURPOSES.

LUNCH BILL SEEMS UNUSUALLY HIGH. WIFE DID NOT EAT WITH HIM. DRINKS DURING HIS LUNCH. THIS MAY BE POSSIBLE CAUSE OF HIS POOR PRODUCTIVITY DURING AFTERNOON WORK DAYS.

PHONE NUMBER 772-3461 BELONGS TO LULU ROCKET. SECOND CALL TODAY TO THIS NUMBER.

BOUGHT VERY EXPENSIVE LINGERIE AT EXCLUSIVE WOMAN'S STORE. NOT HIS WIFE'S SIZE.

BOUGHT BOTTLE EXPENSIVE CHAMPAGNE. HE USUALLY BUYS BOURBON OR RUM. MUST BE SPECIAL OCCASION.

LEFT WORK AT 4:10. PURCHASED CHAMPAGNE AT LIQUOR STORE 2 MILES FROM WORK AT 4:25.

BOUGHT NEWSPAPER AT 7:25 NEAR HIS HOUSE. UNACCOUNT-ABLE 3 HOURS.

Cards such as this may one day allow people to purchase merchandise or services and have the cost automatically deducted from their checking accounts.

shops by using a special plastic card. The card is inserted into a reading device at the shop, and an automatic credit to the merchant's account at the bank and an automaic debit to the customer's account is made. The customers can also choose to have the debits to their accounts delayed 35 days. Under this arrangement, the merchant still has his account credited immediately. After the 35 days, the customer's account is debited automatically. If an overdraft results, the amount due is automatically converted into a bank loan at 12-percent annual interest.

From a technical point of view, there is little question that it will become possible to execute, electronically, financial transactions within fractions of a second over any distance. The key problem, however, is what protection against fraud can be obtained. Even without automatic features to transfer funds, credit cards are already causing widespread concern as a result of fraudulent use. Once these cards are inserted into cash registers and the amounts deducted electronically from the card owner's checking account, the opportunities for fraud will clearly multiply.

Criminals have begun to use stolen credit cards instead of guns—the cards are safer and produce a good return. In the New York area, a stolen card sells for $75 to $200, depending on the company that issued it, how long the card has to go, and whether or not it has been signed by the rightful owner. The typical loss on a card that is known to have been stolen is $500 to $7,000. Unless computer-controlled card-checking systems are implemented soon, many credit card companies may be forced out of business.

With most credit card companies the owner's liability is limited to $50.00 for a lost or stolen credit card. The credit card company thus stands to lose considerable money whenever a card is used without authorization. In a cashless-checkless system, however, the owner himself may stand to suffer substantial loss whenever the card is used. Of course, an unauthorized transaction could be automatically stopped if the system is informed that the card had been lost or stolen and was being used without permission.

The question still remains. Will greenbacks and checks be replaced by electronic pulses and bits? While traditionally "two bits" have been worth 25¢, in an electronic environment two bits can easily represent 2 million dollars. It is this consideration that presents a threat to security and a temptation for fraud. Obviously, further expansion of the cashless-checkless system will be limited until anti-fraud measures can be effectively implemented.

How Well Do We Apply Computers?

It is important to remember that computer technology is in its earliest stages. Compared with aviation, for example, we are still in the 1920's. The day will come when some of today's most advanced computers will be in museums.

The acquisition, processing, and communication of data are fundamental to continuing human progress. We will probably never reach an acceptable plateau of development. If and when computer technology levels off or begins to decline, then, inevitably, civilization will follow the same trend.

Our goal, therefore, must be constant improvement. This means focusing on obvious problem areas and exploiting each new technological breakthrough. Our objective is to mold computer applications to meet the needs of society. The computer will be of little value until it is utilized to fill human needs and to help solve human problems.

At present, we have only begun to use computers. If we have failed in some ways during the past 28 years, it has been in a lack of emphasis upon the optimization of computer use and the development of more usable and understandable human-machine interfaces.

In fundamental terms, the computer is an extension of man's intellectual capacity. If a thought process can be identified, regardless of the field of endeavor, there will always be a potential benefit in following it through by the application of a computer. In the remaining chapters of this book the reader will discover how the computer is used in hundreds of applications.

Recommended Reading

Dorf, R.C., *Introduction to Computers and Computer Science,* Boyd & Fraser, 1972, Chaps. 12 and 18.

Gerald, C.F., *Computers and the Art of Computation,* Addison-Wesley, 1972, Chap. 15.

Martin, J., and Norman, A.R.D., *The Computerized Society,* Prentice-Hall, 1970.

Computers and Society, Nikolaieff, G. A., ed., H. W. Wilson, 1970.

Rothman, S., and Mosmann, C., *Computers and Society,* Science Research Associates, 1972, Chap. 1.

3

Computers in Medicine

The Need for Computers in Medicine

Medicine is facing the problem of information overload similar to that being faced by many areas of society today. Doctors and hospitals are no longer capable of effectively handling the tremendous flood of information about medical research and patient care. The medical profession desperately needs a method to store and process their vital data in a manner meaningful to the medical community and helpful to the patient.

In recent years there have been signs of the computer becoming one solution to their problem. What exactly does this statement mean? Will a computer—instead of a doctor—diagnose our illnesses? Is it possible that computers will replace the family physician? The answers to such questions should be obvious. Computers can *help* a doctor to diagnose a disease, but remarkable as they may be, they are merely machines. In medicine, a computer is simply another tool, like a microscope or stethoscope, that can help a doctor do a better job.

There are many uses for computers in medicine. They can help make more medical care available in the face of an apparently inevitable and progressive decrease in the number of trained doctors, nurses, and other health personnel. They can help doctors keep abreast of important new advances and thus improve the quality of medical care. They may even extend the frontiers of medicine by helping medical research conquer some of today's diseases.

Medicine is still a few years behind business and industry in making large-scale use of computers. However, the 1970's should change that situation. The machines will be increasingly used to

- Study heart disease, cancer, and many other ills
- Analyze brain waves and thus increase knowledge about fatigue, stress, and mental illness
- Guide the management of handicapped persons

· Help perform the administrative functions in hospitals
· Provide early warning profiles of mentally ill patients
· Help train doctors and health personnel
· Free doctors and nurses to spend more time with patients
· Monitor pulse, temperature, blood pressure, and other vital clinical facts about critically ill patients
· Provide immediate information to aid diagnosis and treatment of accidental-poisoning victims
· Help speed processing of hospital patients' laboratory tests

In detail, some of the functions of computers are as follows:

— *Heart disease.* By means of delicate sensing devices, the heart patient can be "hooked up" with thin wires to a computer. Result: continuous monitoring of his blood pressure, heart beat, blood flow, temperature, and fluid balance. If an emergency should occur, doctors and nurses can save precious moments in effecting life-saving therapeutic measures.

— *Mental illness.* Fed with data about mental patients, a computer can formulate an "early warning profile." This reveals characteristics of patients who may become violent or self-destructive; thus the computer can help predict and prevent dangerous behavior before it occurs.

— *Shock.* This little-understood threat to life may be caused by blood loss, injury, burns, or overwhelming infection. At the University of Southern California School of Medicine, a computer "watches" shock patients constantly. It provides instant medical information on 24 vital body functions and helps doctors treat shock with the speed and precision it urgently requires.

Diagnosis. Obviously no machine can replace a person—if that person is a physician with years of experience and judgment—in diagnosing the ills of a tremendously varied group of patients. However, a computer can provide invaluable diagnostic help for the doctor. Many times computers have picked out "gray areas" in a questionable diagnosis. The machine can point to possible flaws and in seconds can provide reams of information from its own memory bank—information which may help confirm or deny the physician's evaluation of a difficult or puzzling case.

One may think of the computer as a never-tiring assistant to medical personnel. It is capable of doing an unbelievable amount of routine work that doctors and nurses usually have to do. It can also perform complex data collection and compare operations in a way that may often aid surgeons in their work.

For example, at the Texas Institute for Research and Rehabilitation (TIRR) at Baylor University, doctors needed to solve this problem: How long should patients with abnormal spinal curvature remain in casts after the spine has been straightened? If the cast is removed too soon, the spine tends to return to its original position. If it is left on too long, other organs and body systems may suffer. A computer analyzed the data collected from many patients and gave doctors the answer: *The cast should be removed after 12 to 16 weeks.*

Computer work by the Texas researchers has enabled doctors to predict whether a patient with nerve or muscle damage will recover muscle strength quickly or slowly. Moreover, computers at TIRR have also shown that children with cystic fibrosis, an inherited disorder that affects lungs and digestion, suffered less stunting of growth if lung infection was controlled and if they underwent oxygen-enriched deep-breathing exercises several times a day.

In a computer system installed at the State University of New York (Downstate Medical Center, Brooklyn), the frustrations of a simple visit to the outpatient section have been greatly minimized. The computer:

- Makes your appointment so that you see a doctor within a very few minutes after you appear at the hospital.
- Selects the proper examining room for your particular medical problem.
- Alerts the laboratory, X-ray department, and other diagnostic facilities so that you can receive service within three minutes at each.
- Makes sure that any prescriptions you require will reach you within a few minutes.

By 1980, a large majority of hospitals will use computers for both administrative and patient care functions.

Let us now take a closer look at some of the uses of computers in the medical field.

Hospital Administration

In hundreds of hospitals across the country the newest participant in the health business is not a new wing to the building or the latest radiology unit. It is a computer. Hospital administrators use computers to process information needed to run the hospital and to supply reports to government agencies.

The most common functions to be computerized in hospitals are business-oriented: accounting, payroll, billing, inventory control. The computer performs inventory control in a hospital—keeping track of drugs, supplies, and so forth—much as it performs control in a warehouse or factory. Hospital bed accounting is an important application for computers. Getting a patient into the hospital and into a bed is every bit as important as getting him efficiently discharged. This task seems easy enough until the volume of patient traffic is considered—29 million admissions to some 8,000 hospitals in a single year.

Boston's Children's Hospital (54 clinics) has been using a computerized bed scheduling and clinic appointment system since 1966. Display terminals (linked to a computer) are located in the reception area of the outpatient building and on each floor of the building housing the clinics. When a child is brought for an appointment, a clerk uses the computer-controlled system to display the next available openings (dates and unfilled time slots) for that

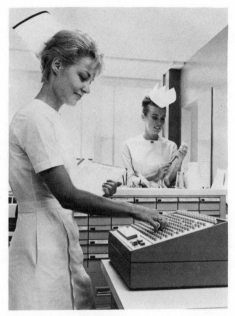

A keyboard terminal in use for drug inventory and other administrative functions. (*Courtesy,* IBM Corp.)

particular clinic. A convenient time is chosen, and if several clinic stops have to be made, it is possible to consolidate appointments all in one day, eliminating return trips.

Hospital administrators have continually sought ways to ensure that all charges for tests, drugs, and other services are accurately recorded so that billing will reflect the true cost of the patient's hospital stay. The computer is lending a hand in this procedure, but the real key to successful cost accounting and billing is the capturing of cost information at the source and at the time the cost is incurred. There are several devices that can be used for this purpose. Information contained on punched cards, describing the service or drug, along with the patient's identity, can be transmitted to the computer. The computer immediately calculates and records the charge for the service. Prepunched plastic cards and keys on a touch-tone telephone can also be used to transmit charges for services performed in various departments to a central collection station.

The scope of a patient accounting system generally includes census, billing, and accounts receivable. These subsystems are described as follows:

Census The census serves as a communications link between nursing stations and ancillary departments. Census reports may also be used to report vital signs and other nursing data. In addition, census data frequently supplies reports for official medical records and keeps the staff advised of pending Medicare certifications.

Hospital accounting reports provide administration with data necessary to run
a complex hospital efficiently.

Billing The patient billing program posts charges to the patient's account
and prepares his bill. Many systems offer an insurance proration feature in which
the computer estimates that portion of the bill which is due from third party
carriers. The billing subsystem also collects and reports utilization data and
provides a management-oriented analysis of revenue data.

Accounts receivable The accounts receivable reports assist the collection
efforts of the hospital's business office.

A patient accounting system allows a hospital to automate many administrative
tasks and thus reduce outstanding accounts receivable, trim clerical staff costs,
and eliminate many statistical chores associated with census tabulations and
Medicare cost reporting.

Diagnostic Assistance

One of the newest and most exciting uses for the computer is in the
diagnosis of disease. It provides a ready storehouse of possibly relevant informa-

tion for use by physicians. Seated at typewriter-like or display consoles, they can direct questions to the computer and receive the information they need to make diagnostic judgments.

In a typical exchange with a computer, a physician might type in a few symptoms, and the computer would respond by printing out a list of possible diseases. The physician might then ask why a particular disease appears on the list, and the computer would supply a number of possible cause-and-effect relationships. The physician could then ask for more information about a particular causal path, examine the logic, and agree or disagree with the computer's response. Searching in this way, the doctor could make a logical examination of all the possibilities stored in the machine. Busy doctors who treat hundreds of patients will find this new system a tremendous timesaving tool.

The computer could also be programmed to give the doctor a list of possible treatments and the latest drugs that may serve to restore the patient to health.

The potential value of the computer as a diagnostic aid has been studied in a wide variety of situations. The first practical study to appear was that of Dr. Homer Warner and his colleagues in 1961. They applied a machine to the differential diagnosis of congenital heart disease, a field that often poses particularly difficult problems even to the expert. Data on 53 symptoms and signs pertaining to children with 32 different forms of congenital heart disease were fed into the machine. A group of new patients was then studied. It was found that the diagnosis calculated by the computer agreed with the actual condition (found at the time of operation or by cardiac catheterization studies) at least as often as did the diagnosis of three *experienced cardiologists.* Presumably, therefore, the machine performs better than would a doctor inexperienced in handling children with congenital heart disease.

By following a simple checklist of questions on a pro-forma sheet, the inexperienced doctor can generate the data that the machine needs. The computer program thus enables all doctors to arrive at correct diagnoses; it allows the accumulated experience of a few experts to be available to all.

Although the old country doctor was said to be able to diagnose an illness as soon as he walked into the patient's room, it is doubtful if any doctor could retain and recall all the information needed today for instant diagnosis of *all* diseases and illnesses. Furthermore, medical knowledge is now increasing at a faster rate than most physicians' ability to keep up with it. Only a computer can be expected to retain and recall all stored information on diseases and illnesses. Working with a computer, a doctor can make use of not only his own knowledge but also the knowledge of the specialists who placed the data into the computer. Let us take a look at a few examples.

The neurological department of M.I.T. is directing a project that involves three Boston hospitals. These hospitals are operating one of the first remote computerized medical diagnostic systems. Linked by telephone lines with each institution, a computer processes information from electrocardiograms as well as from eye movement and hand motor-coordination studies. After the data is processed, it is presented in graphical and other forms for use by physicians. Hopefully it will help them understand why certain malfunctions develop.

A new degree of accuracy in pinpointing mental illnesses, predicting how long patients will stay in hospitals, and foreseeing behavior patterns is being achieved by psychiatrists with the aid of a computer. Physicians at five Missouri hospitals interview patients and transmit preliminary figures via computer terminals to a central computer. The computer compares this information with a vast file of psychiatric data and reports back (1) the three most likely afflictions in their most probable order; (2) the likelihood of the individual's remaining a patient more or less than 90 days; and (3) his possible tendencies to commit suicide or assault or to run away.

This program has compiled more than 100,000 case histories. Now, when a physician submits preliminary findings and his own diagnosis, he, in effect, gains access to the system's extensive, standardized file of demographic, mental, behavioral, and historical information—a body of knowledge he never could accumulate in his own mind.

The system recommends its diagnosis from the eight illnesses—ranging from neurosis to schizophrenia—that affect 95 percent of all mental patients. It has correctly suggested the possibility of long-term treatment in 75 percent of the cases.

Patient Monitoring

Patients can be continuously monitored by scanning units connected to a computer. Processing may occur in either *off-line* or *on-line* mode.* The off-line data can be recorded by the physician or nurse on special cards or forms (or at appropriate terminals) and then fed into computer storage as part of the basic patient record. The on-line data, such as electrocardiograms and respiration rates, can be automatically monitored by the computer and directly fed into storage without human intervention once the original man-machine connection has been made.

Patient monitoring can take place in three general areas: the operating room (O.R.), the recovery room, and the ward. Monitoring needs are very much a function of the environment in question. In the post-operative and intensive-care ward, just a few parameters usually need to be monitored, although these typically change from case to case. In the O.R., more extensive monitoring is usually required, including determination of difficult-to-measure bodily functions and states through computations carried out on more easily measurable quantities.

---

*A part of a computer system is *on-line* if it is directly connected to the computer. *Off-line* equipment is not connected to the computer.

One of the earliest projects to develop an on-line system for direct patient monitoring was initiated at the Shock Research Unit of the University of Southern California's School of Medicine and the Los Angeles County Hospital. An automatic digital monitoring system has been assembled that monitors 24 variables, including blood pressure, respiration rate, heart rate, body temperature, cardiac output, venous pressure, and urine output. Two patients can be monitored simultaneously 24 hours a day. The primary measurements are processed by a computer, and the measured and derived variables are printed out on a typewriter in the ward and displayed on a screen at the patient's bedside. In addition, cards are punched for subsequent off-line analysis of data. The purpose of this effort is to improve efficiency in the care of the seriously ill and explore basic physiological factors relating to shock and circulatory failure.

Monitoring needs can be very diverse. Close to 90 percent of all hospital patients need no monitoring whatsoever during the course of their stay but where it is useful, constant monitoring can be very important. For example, estimates indicate that nearly half of the coronary patients who die in hospitals could be saved through monitoring.

At the Pacific Medical Center in San Francisco, a computer monitors the condition of five patients simultaneously. Simultaneously, it runs extensive analysis on the readings, displays a broad range of data in both alphanumeric and graphic form, and responds to special requests for analyses. The results of all analyses are automatically displayed on a television monitor. They can also be produced in the form of hard-copy time plots on a strip chart recorder. At the end of each day, the system produces a 24-hour log of all activity. It also plots the behavior of the variables monitored against time.

The system also performs alarm functions by generating sound and flashing visual signals when variables exceed high-low limits. Four categories of variables are measured: temperature, heart, respiration and blood. Temperature is monitored through three variables: the internal and skin temperature of the patient and the ambient temperature of the room. Heart action is monitored through two variables: heart rate and rate of premature ventricular contractions (PVC). More than a dozen major variables are used to monitor the respiratory system. The circulatory system is monitored through fourteen variables. Many of these variables are obtained from sensors attached to the patient.

Specialists at the Cox Heart Institute use a computer to predict adverse changes in the condition of cardiac patients. This monitoring system is linked to heart patients at Kettering Hospital in Dayton, Ohio by means of bedside sensing devices. Measured results are continuously transmitted to the computer which compares them every 20 seconds to what is considered acceptable or normal under the circumstances. In the event of any abnormal trends, the computer displays this information on a nurses' central monitoring console. The nurse may then alert the attending physician or take other corrective action.

How about having a baby with the aid of a computer? Well not exactly, but doctors in a European hospital are using a patient monitoring system to predict childbirth. During the crucial moment, doctors at the hospital use an intrauterine catheter and train gauge to monitor contractions, and a skin electrode and cardiotachometer to take the fetal heart-rate. The computer is programmed to produce a visual display which is shown via a closed circuit TV set near the patient's bed.

Computerized Electrocardiography

An *electrocardiogram* (ECG) is a record, taken from the body surface, of variations in electrical potential produced by the heart. The muscular activity or pumping action of the heart is related to an inward and outward flow of ions through membranes of the heart muscle. These alternating or pulsating flows of ions precede muscular contraction and relaxation. The resultant of these various waves with their combined strength and direction is called the electrical axis of the heart. The electrical axis is affected by the patient's present physique and the condition of the heart, whether normal or damaged or diseased. Alteration of any segments of the heart will produce a corresponding change to the electrical axis of the heart, as well as to the vital parameters measured. Analysis of the component parts (waves) that make up the electrical axis of the heart will reveal the location of the damaged area.

The electrocardiogram waveform plot is determined by attaching a number of small transducers to the patient's chest. (A transducer is a device that transforms mechanical motion into proportional electrical signals.) The physician, usually a *cardiologist,* inspects the waveforms to determine if the heart is healthy. The reading and interpretation of large numbers of electrocardiograms is a time-consuming task for the physician. Fortunately, computers can be used successfully to analyze ECG waveforms for both normal and abnormal conditions. The computer (1) performs an analysis based on all pertinent ECG amplitudes and durations, (2) characterizes the waveforms from each of the twelve leads of the scalar electrocardiogram, (3) calculates such factors as rate and electrical axis, and (4) produces an interpretation of the status of the electrical function of the heart based on these parameters. The analysis is then printed on a teletypewriter for assessment by the physician.

Visual electrocardiographic monitoring during stress, exercise, and post-surgical states as well as during daily activities produces important information. In constant monitoring, vital information is often obscured by electrical noise produced by deep breathing, muscle movement, and electrode movement. The noise makes automatic recognition of wave changes difficult. Computers, however, can scan such recordings, sift out noise, and measure pertinent changes.

Electrocardiogram waveforms can be transmitted to remote sites via the common telephone network. Using a small, portable electrocardiograph unit, doctors can send a patient's heartwave over telephone lines to a hospital computer located many miles away. Electrocardiographic analysis can then be

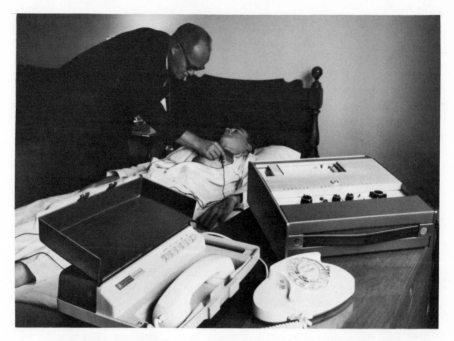

Mobile electrocardiograph units can be used to transmit a patient's electro-cardiogram waveforms to computers located many miles away. Analyses can be returned on a portable printing device within ten minutes. (*Courtesy,* A.T. & T. Co.)

immediately returned to the doctor via a portable teletypewriter or similar printing device.

Computerized electrocardiogram analysis could eventually lead to the mass checking of hearts in much the same way as today's widely used tuberculin tests and chest X-rays.

Medical History

In several clinics and hospitals computers are already being used to administer a preliminary interview of patients. The computer screens the patient before examination by asking a series of questions to which the patient responds using a keyboard display terminal. It has been estimated that up to 20 to 40 percent of a doctor's time and 50 percent of a nurse's time is spent obtaining information from patients. Many physicians feel that the medical history of a patient is the most important part of the diagnosis.

Several types of patient response devices are available: keyboard-display, teletypewriters, film display devices, and the like. At the Massachusetts General Hospital in Boston, the patient sits at a keyboard, similar to that of a typewriter, and answers questions appearing before him on a screen by punching the appropriate keys. In other systems the patient merely has to touch the display screen with a special type of electronic pen called a *light pen.*

Some computer systems have the capability of asking several hundred questions of the following type:

- Do you have any headaches?
- Do you wear glasses?
- Are you married?
- Where were you born?
- Have you ever undergone major surgery?
- Do you smoke?
- Do you have a pain?
- Where is the pain?
- Does the pain occur while exercising?

A system at the University of Missouri uses cartoons to lead patients through a medical history interview. The cartoons shown here are associated with the indicated questions. Still another system flashes questions on the screen of an optical image; the questions are answered by the patient with a light pen. The patient first answers general questions to locate specific complaints, then localized questions. In one case, the patient is shown the drawing of a human torso and asked to show where it hurts by touching the light pen to the appropriate spot on the screen image.

After the patient has completed the interview with the computer, his medical history is printed out for use by the doctor. The print-out reproduced here was provided by a man whose principal medical difficulty was chest pain.*

This print-out is designed to simulate the note that an intern might write in a hospital chart. The statements are constructed out of sentence fragments associated with each response. These fragments are systematically built up into full sentences. For example, positive response to the question about headaches will initiate the sentence, "The patient complains of ... (1) ... headaches ... (2). ..." If the patient then indicates that the headaches are moderately severe, the space marked (1) will be filled in with "moderately severe," and similarly when the patient indicates that they occur twice weekly, the space marked (2) will be so filled in. The sentence then reads: "The patient complains of moderately severe headaches occurring twice weekly." Other responses are handled in a similar manner.

The patient print-out given here was in narrative form. The list could contain a print-out of only positive findings, however, or a chief complaint history (for example, a history specifically designed for a patient with chest pain, nausea, and the like).

After all information has been taken and analyzed by the computer, the print-out received, and the testings completed, the patient sees the doctor. The

---

*Haessler, H.A., "Recent Developments in Automating the Medical History," *Computers and Automation,* June 1969.

MEDICAL HISTORY NO. 0215-0215

THE PATIENT IS MARRIED AND LIVES IN A SINGLE FAMILY HOUSE IN A SMALL CITY. HE WAS BORN IN NORTH AMERICA. PATIENT COMPLETED 4 YEARS OF EDUCATION PAST HIGH SCHOOL, AND DOES PROFESSIONAL OR OFFICE WORK. FATHER DIED OF HEART DISEASE. MOTHER IS LIVING. THERE IS A FAMILY HISTORY OF HIGH BLOOD PRESSURE.

THE PATIENT CLAIMS TO BE IN GENERALLY FAIR HEALTH. DOES NOT HAVE DIABETES. HAS NOT UNDERGONE MAJOR SURGERY. PATIENT DOES NOT SMOKE. HE DRINKS SOCIALLY.

HAS MILD HEADACHES. PATIENT JUDGES HIS MEMORY TO BE PERFECTLY SOUND.

PATIENT WEARS GLASSES FOR READING.

COMPLAINS OF MODERATE, DULL, DEEP, LEFT-SIDED CHEST PAIN WHICH DOES NOT RADIATE DOWN THE LEFT ARM AND OCCURS SPONTANEOUSLY ABOUT ONCE A WEEK OR MORE. THE PAIN OCCURS WHILE EXERCISING. IT IS RELIEVED BY REST. HE HAS NOT TAKEN MEDICINE.

PATIENT'S APPETITE IS GOOD. DIGESTION IS GOOD.

ONCE HAD HEMORRHOIDS.

THERE IS NO FAMILY HISTORY OF DIABETES, NERVOUS OR MENTAL DISORDERS, ASTHMA, OR ALLERGIES.

PATIENT DENIES SYMPTOMS REFERABLE TO THE FOLLOWING: THE CENTRAL NERVOUS SYSTEM, SKIN PROBLEMS, VISUAL DIFFICULTIES, EAR, NOSE, AND THROAT DIFFICULTIES, THE PULMONARY SYSTEM, THE CARDIOVASCULAR SYSTEM, THE UPPER GI TRACT, THE LOWER GI TRACT, THE URINARY TRACT, THE GENITALIA, HEMATOLOGICAL DISORDERS, ENDOCRINE DISORDERS, THE MUSCULO-SKELETAL SYSTEM, AND EMOTIONAL PROBLEMS.

THE PATIENT DENIES THE FOLLOWING: BEING EASILY FATIGUED, WEIGHT LOSS IN THE PAST YEAR, CHANGE IN BOWEL HABITS IN THE PAST YEAR.

---

doctor now has a rather complete report on the patient, past history and current complaint along with consultation-like analysis of the specific complaint or chronic ailment.

Women are sometimes embarrassed when asked questions by a male doctor (and vice versa) and sometimes find it easier to communicate with the computer. University of Wisconsin students can direct VD questions to an impersonal computer system. The computer asks the kinds of questions a doctor would ask and is programmed so that the answer typed in determines what the person is asked next. The "patient" will be advised by the computer of alternatives, such as "It's unlikely that you have VD," "We can't rule out the possibility of VD," or "It would be advisable for you to consult a doctor to get a definitive diagnosis."

Laboratory Automation

Nowhere is the need for computer assistance as critical as in the hospital laboratory. During a normal day of operation, the laboratory is required to accept requisition information, collect test data from laboratory instrumentation, prepare work sheets, generate patient reports, and answer a number of general inquiries for test results. The average time to process a laboratory test in a large, metropolitan hospital ranges anywhere from 40 to 60 hours. In 1970 approximately 500,000,000 laboratory tests were performed in this country. This number is expected to double by 1975.

Many normal procedures in the laboratory are unfortunately manual ones that do not lend themselves to automation. Other procedures, however, can be speeded by using the computer. Clinical laboratories have become the heaviest nonadministrative medical users of computers. The principal area of use is the field of pathology.

Pathology is that branch of medicine which examines the secretions and excretions of the human body in order to diagnose disease, follow its course, aid in its treatment, ascertain the cause of death if death occurs, ascertain the result of treatment, and through research help advance the science of medicine. It includes the disciplines of gross and microscopic anatomic pathology and clinical pathology.

Clinical pathology, in which automation and computers figure prominently, consists of the following major areas of study:

Hematology—The qualitative and quantitative study of blood cells

Biochemistry—The study of chemical changes in the body caused by disease

Bacteriology—The study of disease-bearing bacteria and fungi

Serology—The study of changes in blood serum produced by disease

Blood banks, blood coagulation, and urinalysis.

Of these, hematology and bio-chemistry are primary areas for automation and computerization. In these two areas, 75 to 85 percent of all analyses can be performed under automatic control. To varying lesser degrees, analyses can be automated in the other areas.

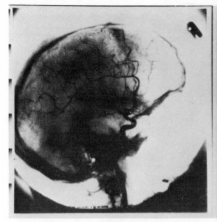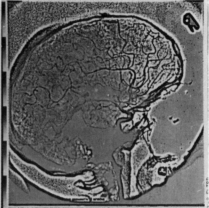

Computer-enhanced X-ray of a human skull clearly showing the frontal blood vessels. (*Courtesy*, NASA)

A properly designed computer system can monitor laboratory instruments, analyze the data to provide continuous control of quality, and relay error messages to the technologists in the event that potentially erroneous data is transmitted.

Many laboratory procedures, moreover, require computations to convert raw data obtained by analytical instruments into meaningful, clinically useful information. Each time a computation is manually or mentally executed by a technologist there are chances for mathematical errors or transcription errors. With computer assistance both kinds of potential error are lessened.

Radiology

Computers are used to clarify the interpretation of medical X-rays. A fully automated radiological diagnosis system has been demonstrated to perform as well as or better than trained radiologists using traditional techniques.

The automated system examines X-ray images, compares the image with known standards to determine the presence or absence of abnormalities, and prepares a list of likely causes in order of probability. As in traditional radiological practice, the X-ray is taken and developed onto 14-by-17-inch film. The image is then placed in an electronic scanner that can examine up to 1,024 spots along as many as 1,024 lines from top to bottom. Readings are recorded on magnetic tape which is fed into the computer.

The computer processes the data into a mathematical two-dimensional array. It enhances areas that require further examination and ignores those which are found to be normal or irrelevant to the type of inquiry being made. The computer program automatically extracts and processes key features found in the enhanced areas and compares its findings with a decision-making format

RAD-8 system shows a radiotherapist how energy radiation will be distributed throughout a patient's body. (*Courtesy,* Digital Equipment Corp.)

developed by doctors at the University of Missouri Medical Center. The findings are then quickly printed to end a process that takes two or three minutes at most.

A detailed analysis of the radiotherapy treatments given to about 27,000 patients a year since 1955 is being carried out by the X-ray Institute of Graz University in Austria, using computers in the university's computer center. Analyses were previously handled by means of a punched-card system. The greater scope offered by computers is already showing dividends in that treatment and dosage can be calculated with greater precision for the needs of the individual patient, based on experience gained with earlier patients. The computer can also be used to provide information on the age groups, occupations, and geographical areas of patients. This provides the institute with the means to diagnose and treat more tumors than was previously possible.

Studies are being performed at the New England Medical Center to determine the long-term effects of radiation on man's heredity. Under the auspices of the Atomic Energy Commission, chromosomes are being examined with the aid of a computer for abnormalities. (Chromosomes are the tiny particles in each body cell that determine hereditary traits.) The percentage of chromosome cells that are abnormal indicates the severity of radiation damage. This percentage is determined with photomicrographs and an optical scanning device linked to a computer. The scanner measures the contour of the chromosome, including its length, mass, and the ratio of its short arms to total length. Using a 35-mm photograph of a cell magnified 400 times, the scanner can measure the film density of 614,000 different points on each frame in a few seconds. The scanner transfers the most interesting of these points—which are like the dots in a newspaper photo—into the computer by measuring the point's lightness or darkness. A report on the analyzed findings is then printed by the computer for review by the researcher.

Chromosome analysis with the aid of the computer reduces the time necessary to analyze the chromosomes of each patient and also provides less deviation in measurement, allowing the geneticists to be more precise in their analysis.

Medical Research

There is no doubt that computer technology is playing an increasing role in medical research. Some 70 or more computer installations exist in medical research centers.

A computer linked directly to testing instruments at the Lafayette Clinic in Detroit, Michigan, is being used to detect abnormalities in the human brain. The computer evaluates information transmitted electrically from the clinic's biochemistry, psychopharmacology, psychophysiology, neurology, psychology, and psychobiology laboratories. It is currently (1) running an electronic counter which tracks radioactivity injected into biological systems; (2) compiling data on the human knee reflex by averaging responses to external stimuli; (3) evaluating changes in the heart and breathing rates under different emotional conditions; and (4) scoring and interpreting psychological tests.

A electroencephalogram (EEG) machine is being used in conjunction with this computer. Responses of the brain to different stimuli are displayed in curve form on a cathode ray tube, and a curve plotter produces an average of the output. Each scan is also stored on tape for detailed study, and computer-printed reports are made available to researchers for evaluation as experiments progress.

Microscopic studies, in recent years, have linked a number of human disorders to abnormalities in chromosomes. At the National Biomedical Research Foundation, Silver Spring, Maryland, a computer has increased the speed of chromosome analysis as much as 500 times over manual methods. Its printed "pictures" of chromosomes are helping scientists locate the causes and effects of hereditary diseases and abnormalities. The recently installed computer utilizes a specially designed scanner to convert microphotographs of chromosomes into digital replicas. The precise digital patterns are then automatically analyzed to

relate abnormal chromosome shapes and shadings to diseases such as leukemia, mongolism, color blindness, and albinoism.

Designing an artificial valve for a heart patient is a tricky business. The cardiovascular system varies from person to person, and the designer's conventional approach is a painstaking cut-and-try method. But a computer technique developed at the University of Utah's Computer Sciences Division holds promise of easing the work. The techniques are useful not only for designing artificial hearts and valves but for studying the flow of blood through arteries.

Without the computer, the designer of an artificial heart valve must build a Plexiglas model of the patient's aorta with the valve in it. Then a fluid that contains visible particles is run through the model and the designer looks for areas of turbulence—that is, areas where the velocity of the fluid flow is changing constantly in both magnitude and direction. This is a danger sign, telling the designer to modify the shape of the valve. Excessive turbulence in a real aorta produces lesions in the artery wall, leading eventually to strokes or internal hemorrhaging.

With the computer, the shapes of the aorta and the valve are outlined on a display screen, and turbulence is indicated by large dense spots. The motion of the valve back and forth in the aorta is observed on the screen. Furthermore the shape of the valve can be changed instantaneously by a light pen and the change in turbulence studied.

Computer assisted research is underway at the University of California at San Diego to determine if the brain rather than the heart holds the key to human life. Many doctors believe that man is alive until his brain ceases to function. By using a computer system and an electroencephalograph, the faint brain waves can be measured and compared to stored information. The computer-determined comparisons can be used to show conclusively whether or not life is present.

Physiological Modeling (Simulation)

The development of realistic models of physiological systems offers much needed help in education, research, and therapy. Researchers at several universities and industrial organizations have developed mathematical models which enable computers to simulate the human lung, heart, cardiovascular system, ear, and blood chemistry.

The University of Illinois Medical Center campus in Chicago has developed a simulation program in which a medical student serves as "practicing physician" to a "patient" existing only in the memory of a computer. The program gives students realistic experience in the critical areas of diagnosis and treatment. Students engage in ordinary English dialogue with the computer-simulated patients. A student identifies himself by typing an identity code and an instruction to begin the program. The computer then introduces a patient with a scene-setting statement which appears on the screen of the display/keyboard terminal. A typical stimulation might begin this way:

> "It is late afternoon on a cold, gray Tuesday in January. You walk into your waiting room and there sits a woman, about 45 years old, slightly underweight, with her hands folded in her lap. She reacts to your entrance by shifting nervously in her chair."

At that point, the student is on his own. He can begin the interview by typing "Hello" on the keyboard—which brings the response "Hello, doctor" on the screen—or by immediately asking any question pertinent to a medical or sociological history.

The student is not restricted to a specific phrasing style when asking the questions. For example, he may ask, "What brings you to see me?" or "Why are you here?" and receive the same appropriate response from the "patient."

The student's question is initially analyzed in terms of 170 concepts which the computer has been programmed to recognize, such as pain, sleep, smoke, weight. If one of these concepts is implicit in a question, the computer searches the patient's file for the appropriate answer. If the student qualifies his question and asks, for example, "How much do you smoke?," the computer will run another comparison through a category of qualifiers. At any point within the interview, the student can cease direct questioning of the patient and ask for reports from the physical examination or laboratory sections of the patient's

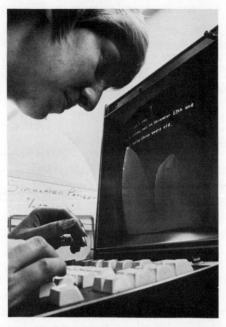

A medical student engaging in a common English dialogue with a computer-simulated patient by means of a typewriterlike keyboard and a CRT display board. (*Courtesy,* University of Illinois, Medical Center Campus)

file. For certain patients, there exists a consultation section from which the student can request the advice of a specialist.

When the "doctor" has decided on a course of treatment, he types his treatment plan on the keyboard. Within seconds, there flashes back a statement describing the effects of the treatment on the patient. If the treatment prescribed by the student is appropriate, it will be noted that the patient has improved and appears headed for recovery. If his judgment was incorrect, the student may be informed that there were no symptomatic changes and the patient is thus seeking another doctor, or, in the event of gross error, that the patient has died. In any case, the student gains insight from observing the consequences of his treatment. The program serves as an aid to independent study since each student's record of performance is maintained for his own benefit.

A mathematician at IBM's Los Angeles Scientific Center has programmed a computer to simulate the intricate workings of a portion of the human inner ear. This mathematical model may help specialists learn more about how the ear works, and might suggest remedies for certain types of hearing loss. The simulation has involved hundreds of thousands of calculations on a large computer.

An experimental lung model, which is expected to be useful both in

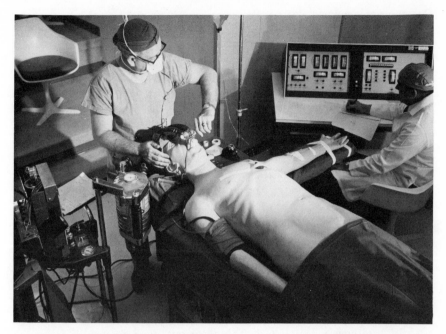

As a student tilts Sim One's head to insert a tube into the windpipe, the instructor varies the manikin's reactions at a console. (*Courtesy,* University of Southern California, School of Medicine)

improving understanding of pulmonary diseases and as a teaching aid, presents a dynamic picture of gas exchange and blood flow in the lungs. This three-compartment lung construction has been developed with data obtained from patients with various pulmonary disorders. The operation of the lung is described by 31 mathematical equations. The model is expected to be helpful, for example, in a type of therapy in which patients breathe different gas mixtures. Physicians may be able to predict the patient's reaction to these gas mixtures and their effect on the oxygenation of his arterial blood.

A revolutionary application of engineering technology to medical education is the computer-controlled manikin patient developed by the University of Southern California School of Medicine and Aerojet General Corporation. This complex medical teaching tool is called *Sim One.*

Sim One is sufficiently life-like to be truly representative of a human patient on an operating table awaiting surgery. Skin-colored, skin-textured plastic covers its frame. The manikin's jaw is hinged to permit the mouth to open and close in more or less normal human fashion. Inside the mouth are all the structures found in the human patient; the manikin even has bronchial tubes. Sim One has a simulated heartbeat, carotid and temporal pulse beats, and blood pressure; movements of the diaphragm and chest simulate the action of breathing; the eyes open and close and the pupils of the eyes dilate and contract.

Computer-programmed electronic systems drive these mechanical actions of the manikin to simulate the symptoms and physiological responses an anesthesiologist may encounter during an actual operation.

Furthermore, Sim One is programmed to provide appropriate responses to the injection of four different drugs, administered in varying dosages, as well as to the administration of both nitrous oxide and oxygen.

While a resident is learning on the manikin, his instructor will be at the instructor's control console where he can monitor each step of the performance. If he wishes to talk with the student, he may stop the procedure at any point and for as long as desired, and then resume from that point or start all over again. Not only is the system designed to allow the procedure to be halted at any time, but also the computer may be called upon for a print-out of precisely what has taken place up to that point. After the procedure has been completed, one may also review a time-sequence read-out of everything that happened to the manikin. In addition to the computer print-out, a pen recorder also charts all vital signs as they occur.

Sim One is used for training resident anesthesiologists in the particular skill necessary in endotracheal intubation. This is the name given to a procedure which involves passing a semirigid tube into the trachea, or windpipe. Through this tube anesthesia gases are administered directly to the lungs while controlled artificial breathing is maintained. This technique, used frequently for major surgery, demands a high degree of skill on the part of the anesthesiologist.

Hospital Information Systems

For several years some people have dreamed of revolutionary changes that will occur in our hospitals as the result of the new computer age. A patient's hospital bed will be selected like airlines select seats for their customers. Meals, medications, lab tests, and radiology exams will be ordered automatically, scheduled automatically, and recorded automatically, as the result of a nurse entering the doctor's order into a terminal at the nursing station. The computer will dial vendor computers so that supplies can be ordered automatically from the vendor with the lowest price for the quality acceptable to the hospital. The computer will store, accumulate, and total the charges for each patient and then print out his bill upon discharge; it will even figure and submit his insurance claim automatically.

Computer use will eventually be expanded to include the recording of temperatures and other statistics. Each doctor on the staff will have a terminal in his office, tied into the hospital computer and set to receive all information about his patients. He will be able to know from moment to moment exactly what is happening with his patients. He will even be able to change orders or add orders, to be printed out at the nurses' station in the ward and thus avoiding an interrupting telephone call. The fulfillment of this dream is not too far away.

A central information system has been developed at the Institute of

Living, a 400-bed nonprofit psychiatric hospital in Hartford, Connecticut, in which the computer has been integrated into every area from administration to clinical decision-making. The computer keeps track of patient behavior, drugs administered, and a long list of hospital medical and business information. The computer also aids hospital training programs by administering tests placed in the system by their directors.

On request, the system can describe in detail the patient's state at admission, last week, yesterday; his medication at every point; compare him with other patients and with normal persons, thereby aiding diagnostic accuracy; and finally turn all this data into graphs and charts that make them dramatically visual. Moreover, the computer's ability to accumulate and process data on patients with psychiatric disorders makes it possible to predict with increasing success everything from the course of the disease to what drugs will probably be most successful in treating it.

Computer-Planned Meals

Patients in one research hospital now look forward to starting their evening meal with a glass of refreshing 1318. That's followed by some tempting 5157 with a bit of 2188 and 1401 on the side, topped off by a fluffy piece of delicious 7106. It's an electronically planned meal, part of a system in a computer-controlled feeding program. Translated from computer code, the dinner cited consists of pineapple juice, chicken fried steak, mashed turnips, apple cranberry salad, and butterscotch pie.

The computer is loaded with a list of all 2,500 foodstuffs in the hospital pantry as well as 800 recipes and 700 inventory items. The machine balances each dish for nutritional value, repetition rate, cost, and other factors. Each main item is prepared exactly the same way every time, thus allowing exact control. The computer-controlled mass feeding program enables personnel to plan a three-week cycle of meals in minutes—a job which formerly took them 80 hours.

Other hospitals have similar programs. Georgia's Central State Hospital expects to reduce its projected food budget by $150,000 by using a computer to aid in planning menus.

Recommended Reading

Abrams, M.E., *Medical Computing,* American Elsevier, 1970.

Ball, M.J., *How to Select a Computerized Hospital Information System,* S. Karga A.G. (Switzerland), 1973.

Ball, M.J., *Selecting a Computer System for the Clinical Laboratory,* Charles C. Thomas Publisher, 1971.

Booth, A.D., *Digital Computers in Action,* Pergamon Press (London), 1965, Chap. 11.

Caceres, C.A., and Rikli, A.E., *Diagnostic Computers*, Charles C. Thomas Publisher, 1969.

Clark, J.O.E., *Computers At Work*, Grosset & Dunlap, 1971, pp. 84-94.

Garrett, R.D., *Hospitals: A System Approach*, Auerbach Publishers, 1973.

Computer Techniques In Biomedicine and Medicine, Haga, E., ed., Auerbach Publishers, 1973.

Knights, E.M., Jr., *Mini-Computers in the Clinical Laboratory*, Charles C. Thomas Publisher, 1970.

Krasnoff, S.O., *Computers in Medicine*, Charles C. Thomas Publisher, 1967.

Ledley, R.S., *Use of Computers in Biology and Medicine*, McGraw-Hill, 1965.

Lindberg, D.A.B., *The Computer and Medical Care*, Charles C. Thomas Publisher, 1968.

Martin, J., and Norman, A.R.D., *The Computerized Society*, Prentice-Hall, 1970, Chap. 10.

Mason, E.E., and Bulgren, W.G., *Computer Applications in Medicine*, Charles C. Thomas Publisher, 1964.

Schmitt, O.H., and Caceres, C.A., *Electronic and Computer-Assisted Studies of Biomedical Problems*, Charles C. Thomas Publisher.

Wartak, J., *Computers in Electrocardiography*, Charles C. Thomas Publisher, 1970.

Zimmer, H., *Computers in Psychophysiology*, Charles C. Thomas Publisher, 1966.

4

Computers and the Fine Arts

When man invented the wheel, probably out of stone, it was undoubtedly rather crude. Gradually, the wheel took on a more finished shape and its use for hauling building materials, grain, weapons, and people themselves revolutionized the history of the race. Man's creative ability eventually discovered more sophisticated uses: the tires of a sleek-looking Italian sports car, the roulette wheel, the ferris wheel, to mention only a few wheels both big and small.

The development of the computer can be viewed in a similar light. The early computers were used to perform rather straightforward applications in the scientific and business areas—payroll calculations, ballistic trajectory tables, inventory processing, and the like. But there is a lighter side to the computer's role of late, a side that is a far cry from the popular view of the powerful calculating machine; this is the role of the *creative computer*. No doubt the phrase stretches the truth a bit, but the computer is now used to help man compose music, produce art, write poetry, make movies, translate languages, design sculpture, make television commercials, design textile fabrics, and perform other creative accomplishments.

Music by Computers

Digital computers have been employed for musical purposes since the late 1950's. While some interest has been generated by the question, "Can computers actually compose?," there can be no doubt that composers already experienced in the instrumental and electronic media have been exploiting the computer as an instrument of musical performance ever since, particularly taking advantage of the great flexibility and accuracy which it provides.

Using a computer, it is realistically possible for a composer to structure all elements of his composition (for example, tempo, timbre, rate and shape of attack and decay, register, and the like) to the same degree as pitch and rhythm. It is through simulating the operations of an ideal electronic music studio with an unlimited amount of equipment that a digital computer synthesizes sound.

There are two main ways of using computers creatively in musical composition. One is to use it for the production of a score. The other is to use it to generate actual sounds (instruments or voices).

The first substantial piece of computer music was produced in 1957 by composers Lejaren Hiller and Leonard Isaacson at the University of Illinois. The piece was called the *Illiac Suite for String Quartet.** It is organized into four movements, called Experiments I, II, III, and IV. Experiment I is a chronicle of "getting started," moving from monody, through two-part writing, to four-part writing. The composers arbitrarily chose some rules of strict counterpoint, an archaic but nevertheless highly codified compositional technique, as the test medium. In Experiment II, counterpoint rules are progessively introduced as the movement unfolds. In Experiment III the composers shifted their focus to the twentieth century with some chromatic harmony, less rigid rhythmic patterns, modern playing techniques, tone rows, and so forth. Finally in Experiment IV, they employed a purely mathematical technique. Experiment IV is an elementary example of "stochastic music," that is to say, music dependent on probability and weighted frequency distributions. The four movements are based on a few elementary symbols, selected at random, with selective composition rules to link them in acceptable arrangements. At a later date Hiller and a different fellow composer, Robert Baker, put together another computer work called the *Computer Cantata.*

Both of these works were generated by a computer programmed to select musical notes at *random* and at an extremely fast rate. The sequences of notes were subjected to several tests, based on established composition and style rules. If a sequence met these tests, and if it linked up properly with preceding and following patterns, the computer recorded the sequence, note by note. Otherwise, it rejected the sequence and tested another randomly generated pattern.

In 1963 Hiller and Baker developed a computer program called MUSI-COMP for generating original musical scores. The program is essentially a way of simplifying the process by which a composer specifies what choices the computer may make on his behalf. *Computer Cantata* and *Cosahedron* were composed using MUSICOMP.

Most composers usually prefer to do their own composing and make their own choices. However, in the generation of actual sounds there are a great many detailed tasks for which the computer is a well-qualified helper. The sound of music is essentially repetitive, a task which the computer performs with great ease. The computer can also adapt a musical pattern to various keys and harmonies.

In 1962, Max Mathews at Bell Telephone Laboratories started developing a sound-producing program. The first piece made public took the form of a record called *Music from Mathematics.* Music IV, a fourth version of this program, was used to produce several of the recordings previously described. Composers using

---

*Illiac is the acronym of a computer at the University of Illinois.

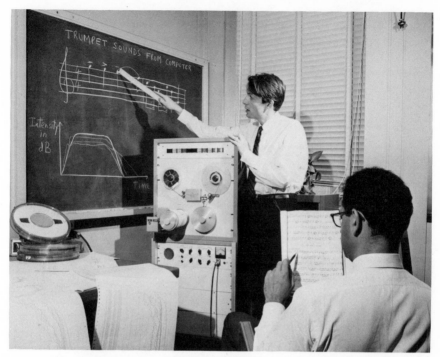

While listening to its computer-generated version played back on tape, a version virtually indistinguishable from the tones of a real trumpet, Jean Claude Risset points out the notes of a Purcell trumpet composition. (*Courtesy*, Bell Telephone Laboratories)

this program design their own *instruments*, form their own *orchestra*, and establish their own *score* that in turn produces electronic music.

A composer equipped with a computer (he might be called a *compusician*) has almost no limitations except his own. He can, in fact, produce his music from numbers selected at random by the computer, in an order specified by him, or by a combination of these two techniques. He can also specify what sounds he wants the loudspeaker to make—whether, for example, it shall include vibrato or how sharply it shall begin or how long linger on the air.

Producing sounds that are as rich and satisfying in quality as those made by musical instruments is not, however, a simple task. Sounds made by a cello, a trumpet, or human voices are very complicated in structure. J. C. Risset, a French physicist/composer at Bell Laboratories, however, has created a computer trumpet sound that professional musicians cannot distinguish from an actual horn.

The possibilities in this kind of application are endless for the composer. He can write impossibly difficult passages for instruments that, were it not for the advent of the computer, would never have been heard. Future computer composers must learn about the workings of computers and add to their

This figure to illustrate the first steps of the computer picture-making process
is itself computer-drawn. (*Courtesy,* Bell Telephone Laboratories)

vocabulary such terms as kilocycles, sampling rates, D-A converter, compiler,
and the like.

The use of computers in music is not a passing novelty, but a logical step
forward in the historical process. So far as the musician is concerned, it is just
another way to express his thoughts and to communicate with his audience. Just
as the development of the orchestra in the eighteenth century led to a Beetho-
ven, a Wagner, and a Richard Strauss, so, perhaps, will the growth of computer
capabilities lead to equally notable composers in the future. There is still great
music to be composed, and the computer will apparently be one of the tools.

Computer Animation

Computers are used to produce animated cartoons, as Snoopy may discover in his next raid on the Red Baron. The whole field of computer-generated
moving pictures is often referred to as *computer animation.*

Animated movies are commonly made by copying a single frame at a time,
a time-consuming and expensive process. Using photo-optic equipment under the
control of a computer is a far more economical method of film generation. The
cathode-ray tube (similar to a TV tube) display, containing one picture for one
frame, is controlled by signals from a computer or computer-produced magnetic
tape. Facing the display face is a camera whose film advancement is also

controlled automatically. This equipment responds to simple instructions to advance the film, display a spot of a certain brightness at a specific location on the display face, draw a straight line segment from one point to another, draw a circle, or draw an alphabetic character. Although its basic operations are quite simple, this computer system can create complicated pictures or series of pictures consisting of simple line drawings or a fine mosaic of closely spaced spots.

A general programming language has been developed at Bell Telephone Laboratories for making simple animated films quickly and cheaply with a computer. Called BEFLIX (Bell Flicks), the "movie language" includes instruc-

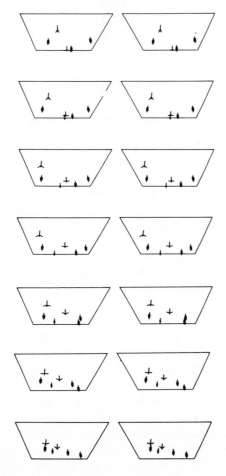

Frames from a three-dimensional animated motion picture of stick figures on a stage. Stage positions are chosen at random, and the figures move at a uniform rate with programmed arm motion. (*Courtesy,* Bell Telephone Laboratories)

tions for drawing pictures consisting of straight lines, arcs, complicated curves, letters, simple geometric shapes, and shaded areas. BEFLIX also makes possible many special effects, such as "dissolving" by gradually "sprinkling" the new picture onto the previous one. Computers can be programmed with this language to make educational films and to generate visual displays for psychological experiments. The film, "A Computer Technique for the Projection of Animated Movies," was completely made using the BEFLIX language.

Thus far, computer animation has been used exclusively for making scientific and educational films. In years to come, perhaps most Saturday morning television cartoons will also be produced this way, not to mention full-length animated features. One can easily imagine the desirability, moreover, of a rapid-film making facility in educational institutions.

Suppose you are teaching a course in celestial mechanics. You want to show the satellite orbits that would result if Newton's universal law of gravitation were other than an inverse-square law. On a piece of paper you would write:

DELT = 1.0
TFIN = 1000
EXP = -3
CALL ORBIT (DELT, TFIN, EXP).

Then you would take the paper to the computation center. After a few hours, you would return to pick up a movie, which you can then show to the class.

In the movie the positions of the satellite and parent bodies are drawn on a frame of film every minute of their orbits (DELT = 1.0) for the first 1000 minutes (TFIN = 1000). The satellite and parent body, obeying an inverse cube gravitational law (EXP = -3), start out in circular orbits. However, as you have shown in class mathematically, circular orbits for an inverse third power gravitational law are unstable. The 1000-frame (42-second) movie drives home the point; the students see the initial, almost perfectly circular orbits disintegrate, with the satellite making ever closer swings about the parent body until the two bodies collide.

Making a hand-animation movie of this sort would require producing 1000 different pictures. At Bell Laboratories in the mid 1960's, Dr. Zajac was able to obtain the above 16-mm film, ready for viewing, within four hours at a cost of about $30.00. In the 1970's we can expect to see a number of uses of automated film-making techniques in the field of education.

Cornell Aeronautical Laboratory used computer-generated motion pictures to study the kinematics of an automobile crash victim during a simulated head-on collision. Boeing uses animated motion pictures in aircraft experiments. General Electric has made an animated movie (in color) of an aircraft take-off and landing simulation system. An art student at Carleton College in Northfield, Minnesota even used a computer to assist him in writing a *movie script*. The computer "fed" him complete sentences that served as ideas, suggestions, commands, and even instructions. Words picked at random and identified only by

"Author — Author —"

© DATAMATION®

their values in an English language sentence were programmed into the computer. From these he got random-choice sentences and used the more meaningful ones to make up the dialogue.

As stated earlier, most work in computer animation has taken place in noncommercial establishments. To exploit the full potential of computer animation will require the partnership of three specialities: computing, film-making, and the subject-matter or technology about which the film is to be made. Perhaps a computer "dating service" can be developed to bring these specialities together.

Poetry and Literature

A number of people have used the computer to assist in writing poetry. A frequent method is to store a number of words and phrases in the computer and have a program arrange these in some sequence which has a random element but is governed by certain restraints specified by the individual. Quite often the computer-generated poems are sheer nonsense; however, poems of some quality are occasionally generated. Two of them by Dr. Guiseppe M. Ferrero di Roccaferrera, which appeared in *Poetry by Computer,* are shown below:*

NOISELESS ROOTS

LITTLE	FLOWERS	COOLLY	BREATHE	PASTORAL	WOODS	
PASTORAL	WOODS	MOLD	PATIENTLY	WHITE	BLOSSOMS	
THE	ROAD	WANDERS	FROM	THE	LITTLE	VALLEY
FIRES	TURN	AWAY	THE	ROAD		

GRATEFUL VISIONS

SOFT	CLOUDS	TERSELY	STAGGER	CREAMY	SNOWS	
CREAMY	SNOWS	WEAR	CASUALLY	BLACK	COLORS	
THE	TIME	BRINGS	AROUND	THE	FRANTIC	YEAR
RIVERS	RASP	WITH	THE	SEA		

Whatever the merits of these two poems, such poetry is certainly no more difficult to understand than some of that written by human poets.

In addition to generating poetry, the computer is also used to perform some detective feats worthy of Perry Mason. Take a classic, world-famous poem that has over 101,000 words and 14,233 lines. It was printed in some 300 different versions. Which version is most nearly correct? That has been the problem plaguing students of Dante's *Divine Comedy* for years. The literary sleuths now have a formidable ally. The National Electronic Computer Center at Italy's Pisa University has broken down the poem with the help of a computer. The result is a volume about the size of the Manhattan telephone book containing tables that list each word's location in the poem. Other tables include an alphabetical arrangement of each word used to start a line, a reverse dictionary in which each word is listed by its last letter first, and a rhyme glossary containing every word that ends a line. With this tool, literary scholars can now apply sophisticated internal linguistic techniques to come up with the version Dante himself wrote.

In literature, computers can be employed to analyze the structure of word patterns. As these vary characteristically from one writer to another, an analysis like this can help determine the authorship of anonymous or disputed works. One such case follows.

---

*Reprinted with permission from "Computers and Automation," August 1968, copyright 1968 by and published by Berkeley Enterprises, Inc., 815 Washington St., Newtonville, Mass. 02160.

Abraham Ibn-Bzra, the medieval Hebrew scholar (d. 1167, Spain), long ago recognized that chapters 40-66 of the Biblical book of *Isaiah* might have been written by someone other than the prophet Isaiah. An extensive international discussion has existed among scholars during the last 150 years as to whether or not these chapters were actually written by a later prophet. The dispute derived mainly from historical arguments, but also concerned the author's style and language. As there was no objective test, no conclusion could be drawn.

A Hebrew University doctoral thesis by Dr. Yehuda Radday has put a halt to the dispute by evidently proving two Isaiahs via computer tests. It has upset theories which resulted from the life-long work of several scholars. Yehuda Radday himself set out on his research project convinced that there was only one Isaiah. He added a completely new dimension to his purely humanistic approach as a Bible and language teacher by acquiring a wide mathematical knowledge while working on his thesis.

His approach was entirely new, applying 19 of the most modern and sophisticated tests to the question of the two Isaiahs. He divided each of the assumed two Isaiahs into three parts for a total of six units and submitted each unit to a series of tests. These included length of words and sentences, frequency and sequence of parts of speech, as well as entropy (the degree of orderliness in the arrangement of various linguistic features). Among the tests was one invention of the doctoral candidate himself—the percentage of words taken from different fields of life such as war, nature, family, religion, and the like.

All these tests were programmed for (1) the Hebrew University's computer; (2) a computer in Haifa; and (3) a computer in Aachen, Germany. The result: On every test, chapter 40 onwards proved to be a sample of writing by an entirely different person than the person who wrote chapters 1-39. Although some tests were more significant than others, a final summary of all tests by advanced statistical methods showed that the probability of the first Isaiah also having written the chapters attributed to the second Isaiah is only one in 100,000. The second Isaiah, a contemporary of King Cyrus, is believed to have lived in the year 530 B.C. and to have witnessed the restoration of the Temple. The first Isaiah probably lived about 200 years earlier.

After helping authors write poetry and analyze literature, the computer is often used to help produce it in book form. The *Long Short Cut,* a novel by Andrew Garve, is reportedly the first work of fiction to be set in type by computer. The text is set in 10-point Videocomp Janson, using the Videocomp and computer system. The type, written with an electronic beam on the face of a cathode ray tube at speeds of up to 600 characters per second, was composed in completed page forms. Prior to the introduction of computer typesetting, the fastest book composition trade was about 10 characters per second.

Here's how the job was done. The publishers (Harper & Row) marked the Garve manuscript with traditional copy signs and directions. This annotated manuscript was transcribed on tape which was run through the Videocomp. The Videocomp read the tape and produced the resulting characters with an elec-

Operator updating a computer with voting developments that are then input to an on-screen display (left). (*Courtesy,* Digital Computer Corp.)

tronic beam on a cathode ray tube and exposed them onto a sensitized film. Corrections were punched on cards and automatically merged into the original tape. Pages were produced at less than 10-second intervals.

One of the benefits of the system is the relatively easy and inexpensive means of changing copy that has already been set. The first setting of *Long Short Cut* resulted in fewer pages than had been anticipated. Harper and Row reduced the line length and reset the entire book, a procedure that would have been unthinkable in normal book production.

Computer-Aided Sculpture

Sculpture is another art form that has embraced the computer. An art professor at the University of Massachusetts has developed computer programs that allow the computer to determine three-dimensional shapes. The program establishes sets of numerical co-ordinates in computer storage which sketch out abstract sculptural forms on a digital plotter. Varying the co-ordinates will squeeze, stretch, or twist these forms in a nearly infinite number of variations. The computer and plotter can be programmed to draw the shape from a variety of sides and a variety of angles.

In Boston, a spheroid sculpture designed by Alfred Duca and built with the aid of a computer is presently located in the Government Center post office building. This massive steel structure has the shape of a many-sided jewel. It was made of Cor-ten steel, a product with built-in controlled rusting, which, after the first year, turned the spheroid a permanent deep red color.

The spheroid has a seven-foot diameter and contains eighty layers of one-inch thick steel, each layer punctuated by 32 points cut in a circular saw-tooth pattern. A computer program produced a paper tape as control for the flame-cutting machine that cut the steel. It actually took four torches four days to bite through the metal plate. Then the sculptor and an assistant spent the next two months welding the 2,560 points of the spheroid to each other.

Other computer-designed sculptures are the "cubes" of Dr. von Foerster and a work conceived by Gustav Metzger, called "Five Screens with Computer." The latter is an elaborate structure composed of five screens, each about 30 feet high, 40 feet long, and 3 feet deep.

Computers can likewise be used to direct the actual sculpting itself. A two-dimensional (flat) view of an image may be converted by program into a three-dimensional image and the result punched into paper tape. This tape will cause a numerically controlled machine tool automatically to cut a three-dimensional object. It is doubtful that this technique—identical to that used to make engineering parts—will ever become popular with sculptors. Few of them would desire a "made by computer" label placed on their works.

Computers and Television

Everyone has heard about computers on television. Many science fiction and comedy programs take great delight in "making a monkey" of the electronic monster. Even the fun of election night is gone; we can all go to bed early because of the fast computer-summarized analysis of the first voting returns.

The first showing of a three-dimensional commercial completely programmed by a computer came on the CBS Friday night movie on April 17, 1970. This 30-second commercial showed a 3-dimensional man explaining the features of a new cordless shaver. The computer had drawn the figure and animated all its movements in a fraction of the time it would have taken many artists working in the traditional animation process (see page 62).

Computers are also used to produce entertainment such as the CBS *Hee Haw* show. Each show is composed of up to 200 segments, all pieced together by the computer. As each segment is filmed, it is automatically clocked on the tape for time length and thematic type. Some segments run only one second, some as long as two and one-half minutes. There are 60 classifications: sophisticated jokes, grocery store jokes, songs, and so forth. Such classifications have always existed, of course, but had never been established precisely until the computer system required a principle of organization. From this base an inventory control system was set up, including each segment's type and special characteristics

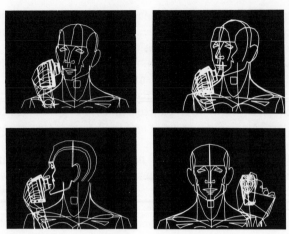

This computer-drawn man represents the mean measurements of one-half of
all U. S. Air Force pilots in 1970. (*Courtesy,* Norelco)

All filming for the show is done in Nashville, Tennessee. By filming one
half or all of one type of sequence for a season at one time—for example, all
songs—the cost of bringing in people and setting up backgrounds is enormously
reduced. The films are then flown to Hollywood where the show is put together.
A request for a specific type of sequence is cued to the computer, which then
prints out what is in inventory on that particular subject. When a segment is
selected, it is automatically deleted from inventory. The computer also keeps
track of the times of the segments considered and prints out the total time for
each show.

Computer Art

Computer art dates back to 1956. Since then, everyone and his dog have
been using the computer to produce pictures. Students of all ages and ex-
students as well are usually highly amused by a computer-drawn Charlie Brown
or Snoopy, not to mention sketches of more eminent figures. Engineers and
mathematicians use the computer to draw pictures of airplanes, electrical wiring
diagrams, bridges, random number patterns, geometrical figures. Research doctors use the computer to draw pictures of body organs, bone structures, X-ray
images. Programmers use the computer to draw program flowcharts. Businessmen use computer-drawn graphs and statistical diagrams. Architects use the
computer to draw building plans, perspectives, pipe and wiring lay-outs. All such
drawings, of course, have a specifically practical value, when they are not being
entertaining like Snoopy.

Artists, however, are using the computer to create a serious form of art.
This art, called *computer art,* is now being practiced in The U.S.A., Great

Charlie Brown as drawn with the aid of a computer-controlled line printer.

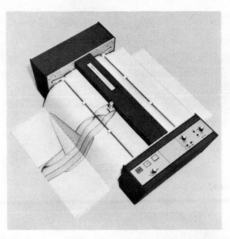

The digital plotter moves a ballpoint or other type of pen in one direction while the simultaneous motion of the paper itself takes care of the other direction. (*Courtesy,* Houston Instrument)

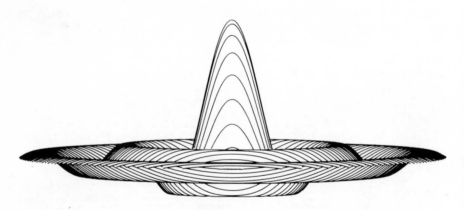

Drawing produced by the digital plotter in the previous illustration.

Britain, Holland, Italy, Germany, Japan, Austria, South America, Canada, and a few other countries. For economic reasons, most of the work takes place at research institutes, universities with computing centers, or computer firms. Probably no more than a thousand people around the world are engaged in this new and exciting activity.

There are three main ways in which the computer can produce drawings. First they can be made with a computer-driven digital plotter which draws on paper with an ink pen. The pen is completely controlled by the computer and can move in both vertical and horizontal directions. Such plotter-drawn pictures are composed of very small straight-line segments which are visible when the drawing is examined closely. The second method uses a printing device such as a

A cathode-ray-tube display showing a computer-drawn Christmas tree. The
hand-held light pen is used to make changes in the drawing. (Courtesy, MIT)

line printer, typewriter, or teletypewriter. This method is suitable for making
graphs or simple drawings (Snoopy again). The third and most desirable method
is a cathode-ray-tube display. This method is also the most expensive.

The cathode-ray-tube display system has a particular advantage in that it
can be used *interactively,* that is, it allows the person using it to alter the image
with no significant lapse of time. Even after his original program is at work, he is
able to control many parameters in combinations of his own choice, to evaluate
the relationships of the forms he is manipulating, and to make use of both
intuition and the knowledge of the problem at hand. It will be seen that this sort
of man/machine interaction makes for a very effective method of producing
bona fide art.

Two of the first users of computer-controlled display devices were Boeing
Aircraft and General Motors. Both these companies have done extensive work in
computer graphic research and have used the computer extensively in new
product design applications. Bell Telephone Laboratories has probably produced
more and a greater variety of computer-generated pictures than any other
organization (its contributions to computer animation have already been discussed). In 1967, Leon D. Harmon and Kenneth C. Knowlton of this organization introduced a unique form of computer art. Using a special technique, they
produced a 12-foot long picture of a nude, a telephone, seagulls, and a gargoyle.
Their technique is described below.*

---

*Harmon and Knowlton experimented with these pictures (1) to explore new forms
of computer-produced art, (2) to examine some aspects of human pattern percep-
tion, and (3) to develop new computer languages which can quickly manipulate
graphical data.

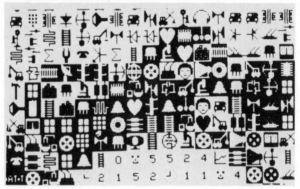

Picture of a telephone composed by a computer-controlled microfilm unit consists of 196 micropatterns, including telephone and electrical symbols, pieces of plant equipment, and so forth (see enlarged detail below). At a distance, these micropatterns fuse together to give the quality of a continuous-tone photograph.

The Fisherman by Kerry Strand, drawn by a computer-guided digital plotter. (*Courtesy*, California Computer Products, Inc.)

A 35-mm transparency is made from a photograph of some real object and is scanned by a machine similar to a television camera. The resultant electrical signals are converted into numerical representations on magnetic tape, providing a digitized version of the picture for computer processing. The computer first fragments the picture into 88 rows of 132 fragments per row. Then the average brightness level of each fragment is computed, resulting in the generation of 11,616 (88 × 132) numbers. The brightness levels are encoded into numbers in the range of 0 to 15. Zero represents white, 15 represents black, and the intermediate 14 numbers are various shades of grey. The original picture is thus

Reproduction of Van Gogh's *Boats at St. Marie* prepared by a computer-guided digital plotter. (*Courtesy*, California Computer Products, Inc.)

represented by 11,616 numbers, each of which represents a small area having one of 16 possible brightness values.

In the finished picture a given brightness level is represented by various micropatterns which can be seen at close range. For example, a brightness level number 5 (light grey) is structured as a house, a cat, an umbrella, or the like. Similarly, a nearly black brightness level (say 14) might be represented as a lightning flash surrounded by a night sky, a white division sign on a black background, or the like. There are a total of 141 patterns for the 16 brightness levels. When a particular brightness level is called for, the computer makes a random choice among the set which fits that level. After the overall picture is produced on microfilm, the microfilm is enlarged photographically to produce a negative which is then used to produce prints. At close viewing distances the many tiny patterns are clearly visible, and unless you know exactly what to look for, the overall picture cannot be perceived. With increasingly greater viewing distances, the small patterns disappear, however, and the overall picture emerges.

A multicolor presentation of computer drawings done by artists and research people is shown each year in the August issue of *Computers and Automation*. PAGE, a bulletin of the Computer Arts Society (special group of

The Mark II Russian Language Translator can translate roughly 300,000 words of Russian into English every day. (*Courtesy,* Air Force Systems Command)

the British Computer Society), often contains many pictures and articles of interest to computer artists.*

Language Translation and Linguistics

For some years, U. S. government agencies have been using special purpose language-translating machines. These machines are essentially digital computers. Wright-Patterson Air Force Base, for example, uses a Mark II Russian Language Translator to translate over 300,000 words of Russian to English per day. Behind this notable feat lies a long history of intellectual development.

Leibniz's *Theory of Monads*, a seventeenth-century treatise, was one of the first attempts to produce an artificial, logical means of conveying ideas. Two centuries later, George Boole, an English mathematician, wrote a book on the

*Since I earlier called computer musicians "compusicians," it seems only appropriate to call computer artists "compartists."

laws of thought* which showed how classical logic could be treated with algebraic terminology and operations, and then proceeded to a more-or-less general symbolic method of logical inference. Troyansky, in 1933, obtained a Russian patent for a mechanical dictionary. These theoretical foundations awaited the development of the large-capacity storage and fast operation made available by the electronic computer, however, for a practical type of mechanical language translation to become possible.

Much of the early work in language translation consisted of word-for-word substitution. It was hoped that the output of such a translation would be good enough to be of use to anyone interested. Presumably the reader's general knowledge of the subject matter would let him fill in wherever the output of the machine was obscure. Word-for-word translation, however, proved so obscure as to be nearly worthless.

The translating computer must thus do what human translators do. It must consider groups of words—that is, phrases and clauses—each word of which contributes to the proper meaning of a sentence. The computer must, in fact, provide a memory span that extends over many words, and (if possible) it must recognize the words as a group. The longer the span of the phrase, the more certain will be the identification of its meaning. What the computer must do then is store words, groups of words, and parts of words (stems and endings). Since this is a fantastically complex task, one can understand why only limited results have been accomplished in the computer translation of languages. It is, however, a needed and worthwhile goal. If we could perfect a computer translating process, a great stride would be made toward removing language barriers. Such a machine would allow the knowledge and wisdom accumulated in the libraries of the world to be made much more readily available to everyone. Sufficiently effective indexing, abstraction, and retrieval techniques, however, may require a deeper understanding of languages than anyone now possesses.

IBM Corporation has developed a Russian-into-English Language Processing System. The system consists of two keyboard-printer terminals, one containing the Russian Cyrillic alphabet and the other the familiar Roman alphabet. An operator at the input keyboard types in a Russian word, sentence, paragraph, or several paragraphs. This information goes into the computer where it is translated into English. This translation is typed on the second terminal.

This system produces a usable, but not perfect, translation. Its stored dictionary contains 150,000 words. The translating program investigates as many as four words to the left or right of each Russian word for syntactic clues that might improve the translation. Words that cannot be found in the dictionary are rendered phonetically into English.

There has been some work on the machine translation of Chinese to English. Since the Chinese language is so difficult and strange to Westerners, it is doubtful if many will ever learn it well. Machine translation of Chinese would

---

*Full title: *An Investigation of the Laws of Thought on which are Founded the Mathematical Theories of Logic and Probabilities.*

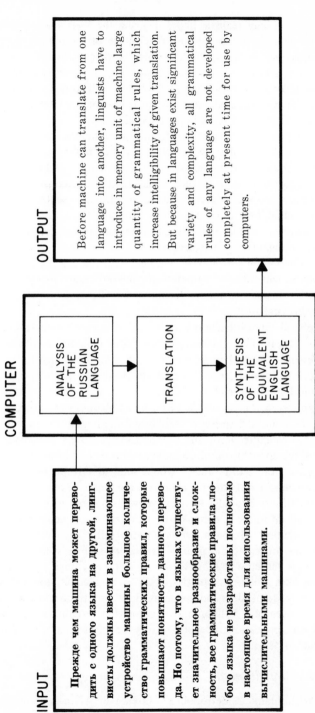

OUTPUT

Before machine can translate from one language into another, linguists have to introduce in memory unit of machine large quantity of grammatical rules, which increase intelligibility of given translation. But because in languages exist significant variety and complexity, all grammatical rules of any language are not developed completely at present time for use by computers.

COMPUTER

ANALYSIS OF THE RUSSIAN LANGUAGE

TRANSLATION

SYNTHESIS OF THE EQUIVALENT ENGLISH LANGUAGE

INPUT

Прежде чем машина может переводить с одного языка на другой, лингвисты должны ввести в запоминающее устройство машины большое количество грамматических правил, которые повышают понятность данного перевода. Но потому, что в языках существует значительное разнообразие и сложность, все грамматические правила любого языка не разработаны полностью в настоящее время для использования вычислительными машинами.

The process of translating Russian (and by analogy any other language) into English by means of a computer.

seem to offer the only realistic hope of giving the West ready access to the manners, achievements, and aspirations of a fourth of the human race, who are currently publishing about 3,000,000 words a year in books, journals, and newspapers. Less than one percent of this vast output is now being translated to English, French, or German. (It is very probable, however, that a much higher percentage is being translated into Russian.) Automatic translation is needed because human translators cannot hope to handle the volume.

Over ten years ago research programs were started at IBM and several major universities. The IBM system contains a photographic memory containing hundreds of thousands of dictionary-like entries, any one of which can be found in a twenty-thousandth of a second. This memory contains exhaustive lists covering the many ways in which words can function in a sentence. It covers all the common ambiguities, transpositions, and hiatuses in word order, idiomatic expressions, and hundreds of special cases of the sort that makes life so difficult for students learning a foreign language.

Only limited results have been obtained with the IBM Chinese-to-English system as well as with others. Automating Chinese presents many problems not encountered in Russian or other alphabetic languages. Research nevertheless continues in this vital area.

A simplified English language has been developed by Bell Laboratories to facilitate translation. This language, called FASE (Fundamentally Analyzable Simplified English), is indistinguishable from ordinary English, except that sentences in FASE can be easily parsed (resolved into parts of speech) by a computer, thus lessening the chance of error.

The expression, "Time flies," would be ambiguous to a computer because the roles of the noun and verb are interchangeable. In addition to its customary interpretation, this expression could well be an imperative statement demanding that we clock the speed of the little insects. With FASE, however, there would be no confusion; the word "time" would immediately be recognized as the noun. A sentence in FASE strictly maintains the sequence of subject, predicate, and object; modifiers like adjectives and adverbs as well as the other parts of speech must fall into line. A complicated set of rules has been devised to ensure unambiguous syntax. Although *syntactic* ambiguity has been eliminated in FASE, problems arising from *semantic* ambiguity still must be overcome. For example, in the sentence, "John throws a ball every night," it is not clear whether John likes athletics or parties. FASE is an adequate tool for communicating a broad range of ideas and it can say almost anything which needs saying. Since long passages of FASE produce a somewhat flat prose, the language is most useful for applications in which clarity of expression is more important than an elegant style.

Computers in the Museum

New York's famous Metropolitan Museum of Art uses a computer for a wide variety of projects: to classify Egyptian pottery, to make chronological tables of an artist's work based on evolutionary developments in his style, even to store all available data on the twelfth-century Bury St. Edmund's Cross, one of the greatest Romanesque ivories in the world. This museum, along with fourteen other New York City museums and Washington's National Gallery, has launched the Museum Computer Network. The network will eventually bank data from all museums in the Northeastern United States. This central file for art—similar to the Library of Congress' file for books—will be an in-depth archive listing artists, titles, descriptions, and bibliographic references. All a teacher lecturing on Roman art would have to do is go to a computer terminal, dial a code number, and have pictures and an arsenal of information about Roman art available the instant he needs it.

Recommended Reading

Booth, A. D., *Digital Computers in Action*, Pergamon Press (London), 1965, Chap. 13.

Computers and Automation (August issue each year devoted to computer-generated art).

Fink, D.G., *Computers and The Human Mind*, Doubleday, 1966, Chaps. 11 and 12.

Hollingdale, S. H., and Tootill, G. C., *Electronic Computers*, Penguin Books, 1965, pp. 268-274.

Conference Proceedings on Computer Applications in Music, Lekoff, G. ed., West Virginia University Library, 1967.

The Computer and Music, H.B. Lincoln, ed., Cornell University Press, 1970.

Computers in the Creative Arts, National Computing Centre, Ltd. (Manchester, England), 1970.

PAGE (bulletin of the Computer Arts Society with material every issue on computer art and music).

Reichardt, J., *The Computer In Art*, Von Nostrand Reinhold, 1971.

Scientific American, Computers and Computation, W.H. Freeman and Co., 1971, Chap. 2.

Sumner, L., *Computer Art and Human Response*, Computer Creations, 1968.

Tatham, L., *Computers in Everyday Life*, Pelham Books (London), 1970, Chap. 7.

Trask, M., *The Story of Cybernetics*, Dutton, 1971.

5

Computers and the Law

Computers and Police Work

We are losing the war on crime. Several million major robberies are committed in the U. S. every year. Crime rates are rising in virtually every category. For example, a few years ago in New York City, there were more than 28,000 reported cases of aggravated assault, 54,000 cases of mugging, and 900 cases of murder. And New York has the lowest per capita murder rate among the nation's ten largest cities. What's worse, nobody knows the size of the submerged part of the criminal iceberg—the unreported cases—in which most of the criminal acts of bribery, graft, embezzlement, and intimidation occur.

Many state and city crime fighting agencies have introduced computer systems to aid police in becoming more efficient and effective. Chicago pioneered in city-wide computer crime fighting by putting the license numbers of stolen cars on a computer in 1962. Now, license numbers can be checked out and identified in seconds. The computer system has since been expanded to include the names and records of over 100,000 persons and vehicles, and the Chicago police feed more than 1,500 questions to the system every day. The answers can warn them if a suspect driving a stolen car is dangerous or is wanted for anything from murder to parking in front of a fire hydrant. Chicago's computer system also aids in reducing patrol car response time. Citizens can expect reaction to a call for help in three to four minutes instead of the twenty minutes to an hour it used to take.

In California a computer now keeps track of all weapons sales as well as stolen property. In St. Louis, all of the city's 900,000 license plate numbers are kept on computers. In San Francisco, a computer is helping collect a backlog of more than $5 million in traffic and parking fines. In Florida, a computer system is cutting communications time and increasing inter-agency cooperation throughout the state. And in Los Angeles, detectives are now putting a computer to work. Clues like nicknames, habitual hangouts, and physical descriptions can be

"As you can see we've installed a computer system!"

evaluated, compared, and identified in seconds to narrow the list of suspects wanted for any given crime.

Similar systems are being implemented across the country. Many of them have capabilities unheard of when Chicago first computerized their license numbers.

Car 54—Where Are You?

Something about the car parked on the shoulder didn't look right to him. The State Trooper pulled up behind it, his turret flashing red, and got out to investigate. As he approached, he saw the door swing open. There was a blurred motion of an arm, a flash, and three shots. The Trooper died several hours later at the hospital. The car had been stolen and the occupant already classified as "armed and extremely dangerous." Had the Trooper known this, things might have ended differently. That's one side of the coin—the tragic price paid by law enforcement officers for the lack of immediate information. But today, the computer is making itself felt in situations like this and all other areas of law enforcement and that's the brighter side of the coin.

More and more police departments in the U. S. are now starting to rival Dick Tracy in the sophisticated devices they are using to cope with the ever-increasing crime rate. Among several devices now being investigated for police use are:

- A cathode-ray-tube (CRT) unit for displaying fingerprints.
- Patrol cars equipped with CRT's and terminals connected to computers.
- Computer-assisted instruction for police officers enabling them to go to a local terminal to verify changes in rules, regulations, and laws.
- Drivers' licenses with holes like credit cards for quick and positive identification via a terminal in the arresting officer's car.
- Mobile sensors to read license plates.

Even without these devices, many police departments have taken giant steps forward in employing the very latest equipment. Probably the most important tool is the computer containing in its memory information on stolen cars, stolen license plates, stolen property, missing persons, wanted fugitives, and similar data. The speed of the computer has meant that officers following a car can now learn within several minutes whether the vehicle has been stolen.

The New York State system is typical of this type of operation. A patrol trooper radios a suspect license number to the nearest police post. There the inquiry message is entered into a teletypewriter and sent directly to a computer at the State Police Communications Center in Albany. Within approximately 17 to 20 seconds, the computer reports whether the car has been stolen. If the car is from out-of-state, the message is automatically routed to the FBI's National Crime Information Center in Washington, D.C. Their computer contains information on stolen vehicles, stolen property, and wanted persons for 49 of the 50 states. A teletypewriter reply is then transmitted to the originating post and relayed by radio to the trooper. Such a system makes it possible to alert a trooper to the facts of a situation before he is committed to action.

A total of 201 teletypewriter terminals are connected to the computer in Albany. Of this total, 72 are based in state police stations, with the remainder operated by municipal police forces and sheriffs' offices. Each month finds additional terminals being added to the network as word of the system's effectiveness spreads among the state's law enforcement officers. An additional advantage of the system is that messages can now be transmitted from one end of the state to the other in about five minutes, an operation that had previously taken as long as four to sixteen hours.

Computers can help catch a criminal by checking on his method of operation (MO). If a series of crimes with similar characteristics is committed, police have the computer print out the identification of known criminals who have previously performed in a like manner. Since criminals tend to operate from habit, the computer often produces a valuable list of suspects. By analyzing past crimes, their location, and time of occurrence, computers can also spot areas of potential future trouble. To make such an analysis, the computer must be continually fed the place, time, and nature of all crimes. The detailed "crime pattern" that this effort can provide makes it well worthwhile for most city police departments.

Law enforcement officers will soon be able to use a computerized system that automatically plots the location of every car on police patrol and displays it on a large grid map of the city. The system will be able to handle as many as 1,000 vehicles and get a new position and status update from every one of them every minute. When the dispatch officer wants to know the exact location of a particular patrol car, he will key up its identification number. His action is converted by the computer into a pulse signal that carries the code for the car keyed. Upon receipt of the interrogation code, an electronic device in the patrol car automatically sends back a return code, consisting of a choice among a number of "status" selections. The indicated status can be "lunch," "directing traffic," "breakdown," the all-important "officer needs help," or any other relevant status.

The patrol car's return signal is received at remote locations in the district and beamed back to central headquarters by a microwave data link. Comparison of time differences from the remotes enables the computer to go into a "plotting routine" that generates imaginary "lines of possible position." At the point where these lines intersect the computer sends a signal to the display unit and the dispatcher sees the vehicle's location on his map grid. He also gets a status display in less than a second that shows what the occupants of the car are doing.

A few years ago an experiment called "Operation Corral" was conducted by the New York City Police Department. The results were very surprising. Using a computer, Operation Corral checked on 183,950 cars in 158 days. Of these, 2,932 were either wanted in alarms for stolen cars or plates, or on warrants as law violators. A total of 165 people were arrested, many of whom turned out to be wanted on more serious charges ranging from narcotics violations to grand larceny.

A recent major fire in a large Eastern city resulted in injury and loss of homes for hundreds of people. As police and firemen arrived, it became immediately apparent that many of the distressed Spanish-speaking citizens spoke no English. An emergency call to the police headquarters led to an automatic search by the department's computer, which held a record of the special skills and qualifications of every man on the city's police force. The names, precinct assignments, and home phone numbers of a large group of Spanish-speaking policemen were instantly printed out. Within thirty minutes, enough of these men were at the site of the tragedy to properly help the injured and homeless.

Police Information Systems

Many states are moving toward total information systems involving all their law enforcement bodies. Such systems would present a police department with intelligence about field units, automatically dispatch these units, display and evaluate situation data, and allow for centralized control and allocation of all resources. This system would also store information about stolen property and wanted persons. An officer needing such information would interrogate the computer directly by a teletypewriter data link. Connecting burglar alarms directly· to the computer would make it possible to investigate emergencies

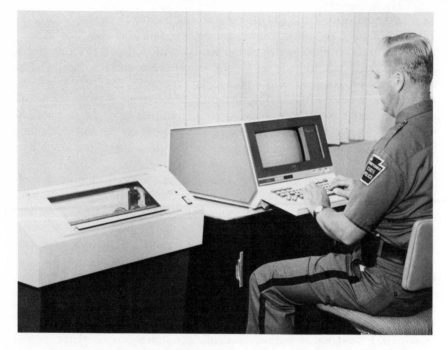

Keyboard display terminals in the Pennsylvania police information system
CLEAN reveal computer-stored data on stolen vehicles, stolen property, and
wanted persons. (*Courtesy,* Sperry Rand Corp., Univac Div.)

without the intervention of a controller. Complex computerized information
systems of this type are being developed by many city, state, and government
agencies. Several of these systems are described in following sections.

CLEAN (Commonwealth Law Enforcement Assistance Network)

Police throughout Pennsylvania use a large computer system to give them
immediate information on stolen vehicles, other stolen property, recovered
guns, and wanted persons. The computers are linked with 291 visual display
terminals installed at 91 State Police posts and in the control rooms of about
200 local police agencies. About 90 percent of the 1,160 police departments in
Pennsylvania are serviced by this system.

In addition to retrieving information from its storage files, the computer
will also direct the transmission of all messages within the network. The system
is also used for obtaining statistical information on crime and for compiling
administrative data.

CLEAN, which became operational in 1971, replaced a teletypewriter
communications network dating back to 1929.

CLETS (California Law Enforcement Telecommunications System)

Law and order in California uses a new weapon called CLETS (California Law Enforcement Telecommunications System). This high-speed message switching system enables any urban or rural law enforcement agency to obtain instant information on wanted persons, stolen and lost property, firearms, and stolen vehicles. It utilizes computerized crime files from the California Highway Patrol, Department of Motor Vehicles, and Department of Justice, as well as data files from the FBI National Crime Information Center in Washington.

CLETS directs a daily flow of 35,000 messages over a 20,000-mile transmission-line network possessing over 1,000 terminals. Two computer systems in Los Angeles and another pair in Sacramento coordinate the more than 450 law enforcement agencies in the system. Equipped with dual computer switching centers to forestall interruptions, the system can switch 17,000 messages at peak hours, operate 24 hours a day for seven days a week, and generate internal messages to send between centers.

SPRINT—A Computerized Police Dispatch System

SPRINT (Special Police Radio Inquiry Network) is a computerized dispatch system which provides the people of New York with rapid response of police emergency vehicles to the scene of critical crimes and incidents. A special New York City police emergency number, when called from anywhere in the city's five boroughs, is answered by one of 48 police telephone operators. The operator, who recognizes the borough by the color of the light on the switchboard, enters requests for emergency assistance into a computer by means of an electronic typewriter. (Non-emergency calls are transferred to secondary operators for other action.) He first presses keys on his terminal to identify the borough, location, and type of incident. After checking a display of this data on a screen, he transmits it to the computer by touching another key.

The computer now searches a file and determines the block number, precinct, nearest intersection, and nearest hospital. This information, along with the numbers of three available patrol cars, is flashed to the appropriate one of eighteen additional terminals manned by radio dispatchers, each of whom covers a specific area of the city. The dispatcher orders a car to the scene, informing the computer of his action through his keyboard. Total police response time can be as little as 100 seconds.

Simultaneously with the display of information at the radio dispatcher's position, information is printed at electronic typewriters assigned to ambulance dispatchers and notification personnel. Thus, any additional assistance required, such as ambulances, oxygen, personnel, or equipment from other city agencies, can be expedited. When the radio car has completed its assignment, the dispatcher recalls the incident to the visual display terminal and types in a

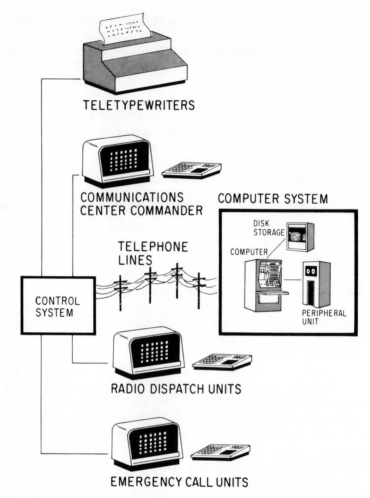

TELETYPEWRITERS

COMMUNICATIONS CENTER COMMANDER

COMPUTER SYSTEM

TELEPHONE LINES

DISK STORAGE

COMPUTER

CONTROL SYSTEM

PERIPHERAL UNIT

RADIO DISPATCH UNITS

EMERGENCY CALL UNITS

In New York City's SPRINT system, computers are used to dispatch police and emergency vehicles to the scene of critical crimes and incidents.

disposition code. The computer stores the record in a completed file for the compilation of statistics and analytical reporting.

The FBI's Computerized Crime Center

The FBI's National Crime Information Center (NCIC) in Washington, D.C., forms the heart of America's growing law enforcement computer network. NCIC currently has a computerized file of wanted persons and stolen property and provides instantaneous on-line replies to over 100 Police Information Systems throughout the nation. State information systems tie into NCIC, while county and city networks link to the state system.

The center maintains millions of active records of wanted persons and thefts. These records are continually updated as criminals are apprehended and stolen property is recovered. Access to the system is via teletypewriter or local computer systems. Normally, an inquiry is answered within 10 seconds, and quite frequently in less than 2 seconds. (Recent policy prevents police units from accessing this system unless their computers are limited to law enforcement and justice work so as to restrict unauthorized usage of these files and thus protect the civil rights of listed individuals.)

Typical of the use of NCIC is the recent case of a speeding driver in Idaho. A policeman stopped the speeding car and radioed the license plate number back to State Police headquarters. In less than two minutes information stored in NCIC revealed that the license plates had been stolen from another car in Missouri, the car itself had been stolen from Alabama, and the driver was an FBI fugitive wanted in California for grand larceny. Another case resulted in the capture of a murder suspect in North Carolina. The suspect, wanted for the murder of his wife and stepson in Ohio, had been the subject of a nationwide manhunt. While driving through North Carolina, he failed to stop for a police cruiser making a routine traffic check. He was arrested for failure to have a valid driver's license, but the check with NCIC showed that he was wanted for murder in Ohio.

Driver License Information System

It was once easy for someone to have his driver's license revoked in one state and another issued in an adjacent state. Things have changed. A system, called the *National Driver Register Service,* stores information on people who have had their licenses "denied, terminated, or temporarily withdrawn." The system identifies the driver by name, date of birth, height, weight, sex, eye color, and social security number. From this data base, the computer system answers inquiries from the various states as to whether or not a driver applying for a license in one state has had his license revoked in another. Today all the states plus four territories use this National Driver Registration Service, which now lists over a million revoked licenses. The Registry handles 50,000 inquiries daily.

Fingerprints and Voiceprints

Identification of suspected criminals through the use of general descriptions and fingerprints is being greatly facilitated by the computer. Physical descriptions and fingerprints (suitably encoded) of known criminals are stored in its memory. After a crime, available descriptions or encodings of prints are typed

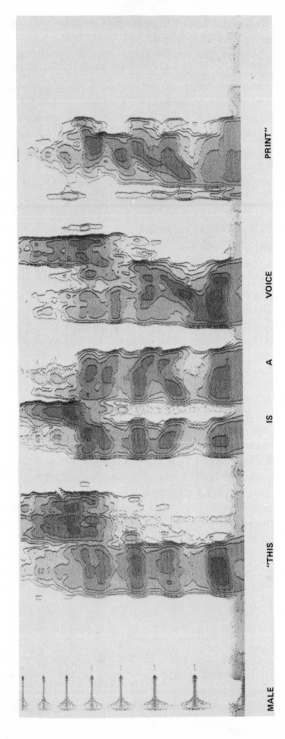

Computers can be used to analyze voiceprint patterns as well as store great numbers of them. (*Courtesy,* Varian)

into the computer. Nearly instantly it matches the new data with any it has on file and prints out the names and addresses of suspects.

Voiceprints (voice signatures) are another method of verifying a person's identity since no two voices are exactly alike. At least one voiceprint recognition system now uses a computer that stores the major features of a person's spoken acoustic signal (for a specific sentence or sentences). One day companies or agencies that require strict security systems will be instantaneously able to verify cleared personnel or visitors by their speech alone. Law enforcement agencies may one day use voiceprint files in much the same manner as fingerprint files are used today.

Recommended Reading

Bigelow, R.P., ed., *Computers and the Law,* Commerce Clearing House, Washington, D.C., 1969.

Booth, A.D., *Digital Computers in Action,* Pergamon Press (London), 1965, Chap. 12.

Clark, J.O.E., *Computers At Work,* Grosset & Dunlap, 1971, pp. 130-135.

Martin, J., and Norman, A.R.D., *The Computerized Society,* Prentice-Hall, 1970, Chaps. 5, 24, and 25.

6

Computers in Engineering

The engineer has been associated with the development and usage of digital computing equipment from the beginning. In fact, the engineer created much of the original demand for computers out of his need to solve problems encountered in military applications. As soon as it became possible to obtain solutions to problems heretofore considered impractical because of the time involved, widely varied applications became immediately apparent.

Aeronautical Engineering

Aeronautical engineering is generally regarded as one of the newest engineering professions, but it is interesting to note that men practiced the art as long ago as the beginning of the Christian era. Hero, a philosopher of ancient Alexandria, developed what was probably the first jet engine. Sir Isaac Newton, in 1687, expressed the jet propulsion principle in one of his famous laws of motion: that action and reaction are equal in magnitude and opposite in direction. In the late 1400's, Leonardo da Vinci, a distinguished Italian artist, drew several sketches of heavier-than-air craft which demonstrated many principles of aircraft design. From the time of da Vinci to the latter part of the nineteenth century, more advances were made with balloons and gliders than with powered heavier-than-air craft. The Wright brothers' flight in 1903 is generally credited as the first successful flight of a powered airplane.

Many early airplanes were designed by trial and error methods. Today, however, aeronautical engineers design supersonic aircraft by the application of a rigorous mathematical discipline to the problems of aerodynamics and structures. This forward-looking approach of the aircraft industry has made it one of the major users of digital computing equipment.

Let us examine how a computer is used in the design of aircraft. Since it is not an easy task to describe in simple terms, let's start with the design of the wing. The engineers tailor the shape of a wing to certain aerodynamic principles and requirements and develop formulas for necessary measurements and calcula-

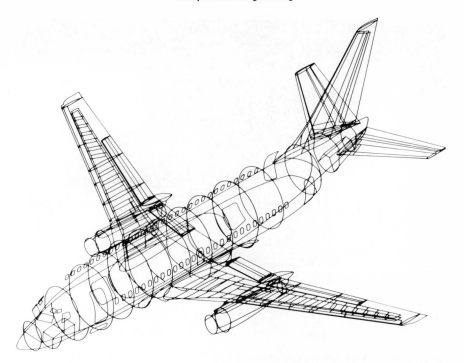

Computer-generated perspective drawing of the Boeing 737 jet. (*Courtesy,* The Boeing Co.)

tions as they go along. However, an aerodynamically perfect wing is an extremely complex thing to describe mathematically and requires an immense amount of calculation. This is where the computer comes in. Engineers no longer laboriously calculate on a slide rule the thousands of dimensions to describe the contoured parts of a wing. Now they simply put their data into a computer and ask it to make these calculations. This is the kind of work the computer does best and more quickly and with greater accuracy than human beings.

Engineers spend long hours with the computer, changing their data, getting new calculations, trying different design ideas in the form of mathematical models. Ultimately, the computer ends up with the exact dimensions of the entire wing shape—precisely as the engineers want it.

At this point, numerical control planners and programmers take over. They make plans for a machine to cut metal in the shapes the engineers have worked out on the computer. The programmers use the same numbers and calculations the engineers developed in the computer but they translate these numbers to the motions of a machine cutting head. Very simply, they produce a roadmap for the cutter to follow, somewhat on the order of the numbered-dot pictures in children's books. The metal is cut based on the engineer's mathematical points rather than pictures drawn (although pictures can be drawn using a

Following an aeronautical design engineer's instructions, a digital plotter draws
each part of the human body as an individual unit, joining one to the other at
the angle of the designer's dictation. (*Courtesy,* The Boeing Co.)

digital plotter). After the machining plan is finished, it is transferred via computer to a punched paper tape that the cutting machine reads in the same way a
player piano reads a punched music roll. Parts are machined exactly along the
pattern the programmer called for and in precisely the shape calculated by the
engineer.

The computer has done three things in this total operation: (1) it has
handled the complex mathematical calculations directed by the design engineer;
(2) it has stored a mathematical description of the wing; and (3) it has provided
a numerical description of the cutter path to make the contoured parts and tools
required. Much of the design information is stored in the computer, the final
curves and points are transferred to tapes, and the shape of the part or the whole
is not seen until the tape-controlled drafting machine draws the picture. In short,
the computer is the bright young junior partner and the engineer is the undis-
puted boss. Another way of putting it is, the engineer determines the design
control points and the computer calculates everything between these points,
including the path the cutter will take.

Aeronautical engineers also use computers to design aircraft cockpits and
controls. They must know in advance how a pilot will react physically to a
particular arrangement of dials and instruments. Are emergency controls too

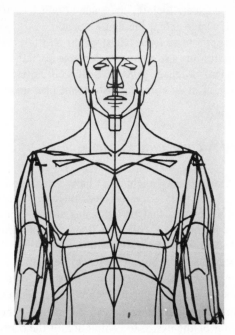

Drawing of the human figure as prepared by a computer-controlled digital plotter. (*Courtesy,* The Boeing Co.)

hard to reach? Are certain instruments in the wrong place? Can movement in the cockpit be reduced by rearranging seats or controls? Manufacturing a full-scale model or mockup of every contemplated cockpit design to get these answers would be very expensive. Having a pilot run through simulated instrument checkout in each mockup would be enormously time-consuming. So, before investing time and effort in this way, design engineers let a computer figure out whether a certain-sized pilot could operate comfortably in the cockpit of a particular design. The computer will show pilot "reach" distances and movements with mathematical precision.

Drawing the human figure in action in the cockpit was the next logical extension of these computer experiments. If all the pilots in the United States Air Force were lined up by height, from tall to short, and by weight, then by hat size, and then by length of arm, the man in the middle of each line would, in order, stand 5 feet, 9 inches tall, weight 162 pounds, wear a size 7 1/8 hat, and have a 34-inch reach. This representative pilot was drawn in seven segments: the body below the waist, the torso, the head, the two upper arms, and the two lower arms. Each segment was prepared for the computer with the same dimensional preciseness used in manufacturing parts for commercial jets. The result is a human figure that bends and twists with unusual realism, despite the fact that it is composed of only seven segments. Each part of the body acts as an individual unit. An engineer dictates the angle at which each part joins another, thus determining to a large extent the figure's action.

Not only cockpits to suit the tallest or the shortest pilot can be designed from computer studies but also more comfortable aircraft seats, better leg rests, and more convenient kitchen galleys. Spacecraft designers find computer sketches equally useful in determining instrument placement and cabin comfort for astronauts.

Architecture and Architectural Engineering

At one time in ages past there must have been a shortage of inhabitable caves. When one of our hairy ancestors coordinated the faculties of his hands and his brain and discovered that by arranging stones, branches, and mud he could create a cave in the middle of a flat prairie, the first local architect hung out his shingle. Today, even though he still builds "caves," the architect uses more modern methods to help him in his work. He is often under great pressure to complete design work in the least possible time. The complexity and scale of many building operations now involve years, rather than months, of design activity before any construction work can commence. The overall period of time, from inception of the design to completion of the construction, is tending to result in buildings which, if not obsolete, are often obsolescent as soon as they are put into commission. The architect is therefore under pressure, not only to speed up the design and construction processes, but also to ensure that the standard of design meets the increasing sophistication demanded by society as a whole. Since the early 1960's several large architectural firms have used computers to help them design and plan building projects; some of their many applications are listed here:

- Drawing maps
- Drawing building perspectives
- Building optimization studies
- Space frame analysis
- Truss and beam analysis
- Wall design and analysis
- Heating and cooling load analysis
- Air conditioning and hot and cold water piping
- Lighting optimization
- Acoustical analysis
- Land evaluation

One application currently receiving much attention from the architectural community is that of space planning. *Space planning* is an architectural phrase

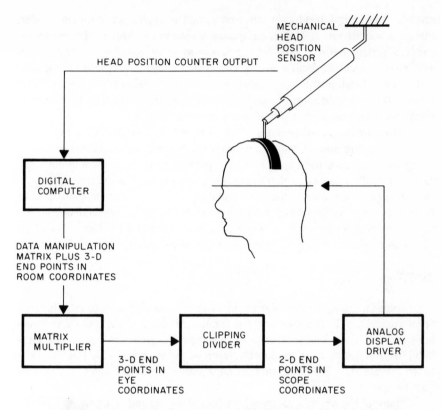

In the head-mounted display device used in computer graphics research at the University of Utah, computer-generated pictures begin as information transmitted from the mechanical head-position sensor and end as analog display data entering the headset.

used to describe the process of locating functional areas within a building facility. These areas may be either rooms or work stations, as in the problem of *office landscaping* (a term used by interior designers to describe the act of arranging furniture and partitions in large office spaces).

Computers are used to generate visual design studies as well as to prepare background line drawings for final presentation renderings and perspectives. Some architects use computers to prepare construction specifications, cost estimations, optimization studies, and planning solutions. Computer-produced maps are used to identify the best location for various land uses.

New computer graphics techniques being developed at the University of Utah may someday permit architects to draw buildings in three dimensions and then visually step into the drawing and view the building from the inside by using an exotic head-mounted display device. A system consisting of a computer, headset, mechanical head position sensor, matrix multiplier, clipping divider, analog display driver, and other equipment is used in this project. The computer builds a matrix defining the head position in three dimensions. The matrix multiplier, a specially built piece of computer hardware, multiplies the matrix that defines head position by another matrix that defines the object to be viewed. This multiplication of matrices rotates and translates the object so that it appears to be stationary as the observer moves around it.

After the object has been transformed by matrix multiplication, the data is sent to a clipping divider, which computes the perspective the viewer is used to seeing and then clips the object to eliminate those parts that he would not see if he were actually standing in that relation to a real object. For example, if he gets close enough to the object, the edges will disappear from view. Images appear in three dimensions when viewed with a head-mounted device suspended from the ceiling. In each eyepiece is a tiny cathode-ray tube (CRT), like a miniature television screen, on which the computer image is projected.

Civil Engineering

John Smeaton, an Englishman, in 1761 was the first man to call himself a "civil engineer." He designed bridges, pumps, drainage work, and other structures and machines. The profession of civil engineering has since developed until today we can see its great monuments everywhere we turn, from Boulder Dam to the Empire State Building, from complex highway intersections to the Golden Gate Bridge.

Many of the newer structures have been designed and constructed with the aid of computers. Several programming languages (COGO, STRESS, ICES, SLOPE, STRUDL) have been developed to help civil engineers solve their problems. For example, the STRESS system enables a civil engineer to write a complete program for the solution of a structural problem even though he has had no programming experience. Such a system affords an economical way of using a computer on a day-to-day basis for the solution of routine structural problems.

The COGO (Coordinate Geometry) language provides the capabilities of solving coordinate geometry problems. Civil engineers at work on surveying, layout, and highway design use certain common terms, for example, *point, line, area, coordinate, azimuth, station,* and *intersect.* With COGO, words such as ANGLE, DISTANCE, and AREA permit them to find the angle formed by three points, the distance between two points, and the area of a polygon, all without writing a single equation.

Each command consists of a name and relevant data, for example, AREA 8 103 115, which computes the area in square feet and acres of the triangle identified by corner points 8, 103, and 115. The engineer using COGO must determine only which commands to use, their proper order, and the data to accompany them.

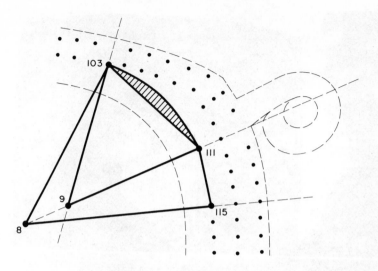

Coordinate diagram for COGO program.

The heart of the COGO method is the simple concept of a coordinate table. Each point involved in a problem is given an identification number (see coordinate diagram). As each point is "located," its coordinates are stored in the computer's coordinate table to be available for subsequent computations by simply referring to the point number.

A typical highway design problem presented to civil engineers was that of the Kentucky Turnpike, which contains many major interchanges. Some of the area where the turnpike was to be built was layered with limestone rock and dotted with sink-holes that posed drainage problems. A computer was used to obtain the following information: (1) Earth-work quantities, (2) slope stake locations, (3) highway cross sections, (4) mass haul diagrams, (5) center line profiles, and (6) blue top elevations for subgrade. This information told the engineers the best location for the roadbed, what grades to give the road, how much earth needed to be moved for alternative road profiles, and how far to move the earth. It also helped to determine cost figures.

Designing a highway with a computer requires nearly constant interplay between it and the engineers, especially in the early phase of the work, known as the iteration period, in which they attempt to arrive at the best road profile. This involves programming the first field information available, analyzing the resulting profile, making changes when better data is available, and so on until the best profile is obtained.

Engineers in Texas are using computers to project the state's current and future highway needs. Assisted by a pair of photoequipped airplanes and two computers, they are compiling vast amounts of information, ranging from projected population growth and traffic counts to the details of acquiring

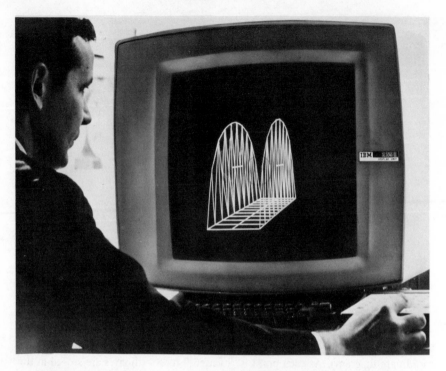

Bridge structure shown on a cathode-ray-tube display may be modified with a light pen or keyboard input while the computer indicates the forces in each member resulting from these changes.

right-of-way and calculating the amount of earth fill needed for grading, not to mention the total construction cost.

Once a strip of area for a new highway is selected, crews in airplanes equipped with special cameras fly over it and take photographs. Each strip is photographed from two different angles. Then technicians produce a large aerial map in which the two images overlap. With special equipment, engineers view it in 3-D (three dimensions). The known reference points in the photograph are used to determine the distances and calculate the elevations of the land and objects. Information on the elevations is fed into the computers to produce cross-sectional maps that show the slope or grade and the land elevations along each possible highway route. These maps and the data compiled enable the engineers to determine easily the amount of cutting and filling needed along each route.

The use of the computer in bridge design is commonplace. Many of the newer prestressed concrete bridges probably could not have been built at all without computer aid. From the engineer's point of view computer-designed bridges have several benefits. Design costs are significantly reduced and design speeds greatly increased; design accuracy is improved and checking is facilitated.

This graphic display system, including an operator display, light pen, and keyboard, allows electrical engineers to design circuits and solve other problems. (*Courtesy,* Texas Instruments, Inc.)

However, it is the contractor who accrues the greatest advantage from the use of computers since they reduce his construction costs.

Electrical Engineering

Electrical engineering is more closely allied to mathematics and physics than to other branches of engineering. It involves the design of electrical devices and systems, including computers themselves. Computer-aided design is an ever-increasing activity with electrical engineers. Ineractive systems—composed of a computer, display device, keyboard, and light pen—help them design electrical circuits. The designer can see the circuit he is constructing on the display. He can easily make design changes, using a light pen or keyboard, and display the new results.

Computers and displays (called *graphic display systems*) are most useful in engineering design applications that involve repetitive cycles of computation,

Display console and light pen being used for computer-aided automotive design at General Motors. (*Courtesy,* General Motors Corp.)

analysis and parameter variation. For example, in designing an electronic circuit, the engineer may draw the circuit schematics on the display and enter the value of each component via the keyboard. The voltage waveform produced by the circuit can be displayed beside the circuit diagram. Using the light pen the engineer may then insert a new parameter value or delete or add a component. The new waveform resulting from the new circuit will be immediately displayed. Iterations can be continued in this fashion until the engineer arrives at an optimized design.

Engineers also use computers to design other computers. They check logic, describe circuits, allocate interconnection points, route wires, produce punched cards to run wire-wrap machines, and help program tape-controlled drilling operations. The use of computers in the design and production of new computers and other devices is called *design automation.*

Mechanical Engineering

Mechanical engineering relates specifically to power and mechanical equipment. It is closely allied to other fields of engineering inasmuch as there is hardly an industry or an occupation in which machines are not directly or indirectly involved. Some specialized branches of mechanical engineering are machine design; automotive engineering; heating, ventilation, and air conditioning; internal combustion engines; and steam and power equipment.

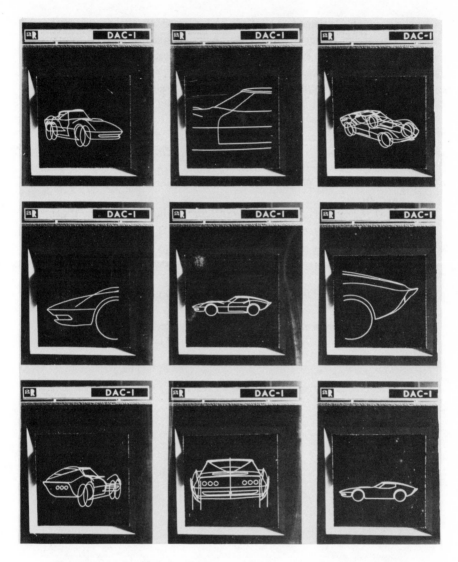

These automotive displays were generated from a mathematical representation of the design stored in a computer's memory. (*Courtesy,* General Motors Corp.)

The mechanical engineer relies heavily on the four M's: mathematics, metallurgy, mechanics, and mechanisms. He has been using the slide rule as a calculating device since the early days of his profession, but today he has a much more powerful computing device, the computer.

General Motors and other automobile manufacturers use computers in car design. One GM system uses computer display devices in which the drawings of car parts can be enlarged, modified, and rotated on the display screen. A mechanical design engineer can revise the design and instruct the computer to rotate it so that he can view it from different angles. The effect of a change in one part of the design on other parts can often be quickly computed.

Engineers also use computers to design and control power plants. Machine tools are likewise controlled by computer. Chapter 9 will discuss the use of computers in such control systems.

Recommended Reading

Booth, A.D., *Digital Computers in Action,* Pergamon Press (London), 1965, Chap. 6.

Campion, D., *Computers in Architectural Design,* American Elsevier, 1968.

Clark, J.O.E., *Computers At Work,* Grosset & Dunlap, 1971, pp. 95-100, 136-143.

Spencer, D.D., *Computers and Programming Guide for Engineers,* Howard W. Sams, 1963.

Tatham, L., *Computers in Everyday Life,* Pelham Books (London), 1970, Chap. 6.

Computer Usage Applications, Weiss, E.A., ed., McGraw-Hill, 1970, Chaps. 8, 12, and 16.

7

Computers in Education

During the past few years, use of computers in academic settings has expanded dramatically. Educators around the world are keenly aware of the impact of the computer and are rapidly working computer education into the curriculum.

For many years students and teachers alike have been applying computers to solving problems in physics, engineering, chemistry, economics, business administration, mathematics, psychology, and other fields. To facilitate such work many institutions are placing remote computer terminal units in key classrooms. Terminal units vary depending upon the department involved. Engineering students have graphic plotting and display units, architectural students have plotting units and graphic input units, chemistry and physics students have typewriter-like and display devices, and so on.

In some schools, the same computer system used for instructional purposes also performs data-processing operations, such as student registration, grade recording, course scheduling, payroll, student transcripts updating, and other administrative duties.

In the late 1960's, John Kemeny, President of Dartmouth College, said, "A decade from now, I would hope that every institution of higher learning will offer all its undergraduates a basic introduction to the computer. Of course, the moment this happens on a nationwide scale there will be many drastic changes. In business mathematics, students will be solving, as routine classroom exercises, problems that in the past only experts would attempt. Plotting a rocket ship course to the moon will be a routine freshman physics exercise. Our students do it now."

Computer-Assisted Instruction

Computer-Assisted Instruction (CAI) can be considered as a system in which a computer acts as an intermediary between students and a body of knowledge, carrying out instructional strategies as programmed by the educator.

"Talking typewriters" used by elementary school children in East Palo Alto, California. (*Courtesy,* Hewlett-Packard)

A form of conversational interaction between students and the system transpires as the computer presents information that has been stored in its storage unit.

Computers can handle large numbers of students simultaneously—for instance, 200 or more—and each of them can be at a different point in the curriculum. In the simplest type of CAI system, the terminal device at which the student sits is something like an electric typewriter. Messages can be typed out by the computer and the student in turn can enter his responses on the keyboard.

Another type of terminal commonly used in CAI systems is the cathode-ray-tube display. An advantage of CRT terminals is that a graphic display may be shown to the student and his own response, entered on a keyboard, can then be made an integral part of the display as well. Some CRT terminals are equipped with light pens. Other types of terminals are image projectors and audio-message devices.

Some instructional material prepared for CAI systems might be compared to a series of textbooks that have been broken down into small units of information. Unlike the textbook, however, the material may be presented to students on many levels of difficulty, and each student can progress through the material on an individual path charted by his previous performance. Communication between the educator (the teacher or person that developed the program being used) and the student remains private, each student advancing at his own pace and level.

At least three types of instructional programs may be implemented with CAI systems: drill-and-practice, tutorial, and dialogue.

The individualized *drill-and-practice programs* are meant to supplement the regular course taught by the teacher. The introduction of concepts and new ideas is presented by the teacher in the conventional manner. The role of the computer is to provide regular review and practice on basic concepts and skills.

Elementary school student using a CRT display and a slide projection device which are connected to a computer system. (*Courtesy,* IBM Corp.)

For example, in the case of elementary mathematics, each student would receive daily a certain number of exercises that are automatically presented, evaluated, and scored by the CAI program without any intervention by the classroom teacher. Individualized drill-and-practice work is suitable for many elementary topics in mathematics, science, and foreign languages, and for spelling, typing, and the like.

The *tutorial program,* unlike the drill-and-practice approach, presents subject material to the student and checks on his progress directly. Whenever the student makes a mistake, the computer acts as a patient tutor and gets the student back on track. As soon as the student shows that he has a clear understanding of a concept by successfully working a number of exercises, he is immediately introduced to a new concept and new exercises. Using such a system allows the teacher to spend more time with individual students having problems.

The *dialogue program* permits the student to conduct a genuine dialogue with the computer. Educational researchers are presently trying to develop programs to make computers converse with their users on a limited subject area in more-or-less natural English. The use of voice recognition techniques in such systems has been considered; at the present time, however, no equipment is available that can recognize spoken speech with great accuracy. It will be some time before voice dialogue systems are available.

A significant advantage of CAI is its flexibility. In a typical CAI classroom you might find one student doing drill-and-practice on Spanish verbs, another learning about chemistry, another studying French, and still others engaged in mathematics, English, history, or physics. Each student is progressing at the learning rate which is best for him or her.

CAI is indeed a valuable tool for modern educators. It is, however, still in its infancy and will not be utilized fully until costs are reduced, better instructional material is available, and more educators learn the procedures required to develop training material.

Computers as a Subject of Instruction

Two decades ago, computer science as an academic discipline did not exist. Today, computer science degree programs are offered at the Bachelor's, Master's, and Doctoral level at many colleges and universities. Many smaller four-year colleges and two-year community colleges offer computer science course work. Many community colleges offer two-year degree programs in data processing and programming. During the past few years, even secondary schools have been teaching computer science courses, generally of a survey nature to provide the student with a broad overview. Computer concepts have been introduced into high school algebra, geometry, physics, chemistry, and business curricula. The amount of usage of computers in high schools depends, of course, on the availability of computing equipment, which in turn depends on the availability of funding.

What is *computer education?* Is it administrative data processing? No! Administrative data processing is not computer education. It is just the beneficial application of computers to the repetitive administrative chores of the college or school system, both in the business office and in the handling of the paperwork required to make the institution function. Is it computer-assisted instruction? No! While there is little doubt that computer-assisted instruction will make a substantial impact on education, this is not computer education. Computer education is the study of information interpretation, representation, and transformation as well as how the computer is used in solving problems. Computer education is learning how a computer is programmed, how it processes data, how it stores and manipulates data, how it retrieves data. Most information about computers emphasizes the things a computer can do rather than what it cannot do; therefore, an equally important part of computer education concerns the limitations of machine organization.

Computer education begins with an appreciation of the immense capabilities of the computer and also an awareness of its limitations and its complete dependence upon human guidance. The student learns how to use the computer intelligently as a tool (just as he uses a library or slide rule as tools). Computer education is the key that will unlock both the potential of the computer and, more importantly, of the computer user.

Physics researchers at the State University of New York at Stony Brook use computers to gather and analyze data on the nuclear structure of materials. (*Courtesy,* Digital Equipment Corp.)

In the not too distant future, most, if not all, students in undergraduate degree programs will take at least one introductory course in computer science. The experiences at Dartmouth College, and other pioneering schools where students and faculty have free access to computing power, show that given an opportunity, students and faculty discover a multitude of new ways in which the computer can be applied effectively. More colleges will follow Dartmouth's lead, and no doubt computer access will become a "recruiting carrot" held out to prospective scholars, especially when increasing numbers of high school graduates have already been thoroughly exposed to the computer by the time they are ready to "scout" college campuses.

Many educators agree that too much specialization at the undergraduate level is not highly desirable; therefore, computer science at that level often supplements a broad educational background. Existing programs at the Doctoral level are quite varied and are largely a function of the interests and capabilities of the resident faculty. The objectives of these programs are to produce students who are capable of teaching computer science, of conducting research, and who will make original contributions in the field.

The computer has a very important application in the classroom in the teaching of the problem solving process. This process consists of algorithm (method of computational procedure) development, flowcharting (pictorial presentation of the logic of the algorithm), and representing the mechanics of problem solution in a computer language. Computer problem solving has helped make the study of mathematics, chemistry, physics, and other subjects a more

Classroom computer being used by students to solve mathematical problems.
(*Courtesy,* Hewlett-Packard)

dynamic and individual experience for the student. The computer has also eliminated many tedious calculations that were once required to solve very complex problems.

By 1980, over 350,000 computers will be in use in the United States. Obviously it will take many people educated in computer use to properly operate these machines. Many community colleges, post-technical high schools, and vocational schools offer programs that help individuals acquire a marketable skill in this area. Business-data processing courses at these institutions are training students as programmers and analysts for working in business and industrial settings. Many vocational courses are also taught at these institutions that will train students to fill jobs as technicians or computer equipment operators.

Simulation

To simulate is to mimic the behavior of one system with a different, dissimilar system. Thus a computer can be programmed to behave like some other system. Simulation is used when direct experimentation is impossible (new system not yet available), undesirable (simulated wars, for example), uneconomical (a process requiring large quantities of platinum but not known to be profitable), immoral (dealing with intentional human death), or simply too slow (ecology, forestry).

A simulation model system implemented on a computer provides students with real-life situations. In chemistry, simulation models have been developed to conduct experiments by simulating instruments and chemicals. In medicine, a student doctor can observe the workings of various body organs. In business, students can learn management techniques by operating a simulated business. In high school, students are using simulation models to learn about major battles of the Civil War, probability and statistics, and even the landing of the Apollo space vehicle. By using simulation techniques, a physics student can even explode a simulated atomic reactor and watch the nuclear reactions in slow motion.

A simulation model is usually a mathematical model of a real-life system expressed in a computer language. Most simulation models used for educational purposes are designed so that the student can enter control data into the model. For example, in a simulated business management system, the student is able to enter quantities related to capital, raw materials, people, production schedules, and so on. The overall objective of using this system might be to maximize profits by making decisions on how to develop these resources. Time is compressed by the computer, so that results of decisions are nearly immediately available; thus a real-life situation of several weeks, months, or years can be simulated on a computer in seconds or minutes.

Another example of computer simulation is a program that demonstrates Mendel's law of heredity in plants. Mendel crossbred plants with different characteristics such as height and color, and calculated the mathematical probabilities for each of the resulting generations of hybrid plants. The student enters color, height, and other characteristics being considered into the program, and the computer uses this information to compute and type out the characteristics of each succeeding generation, based on Mendel's probabilities. This type of experiment would be impractical to perform in a laboratory as it would take several years to develop the several generations of information that are required. The computer, however, gives the student at one sitting an operating example of what Mendel's law is and how it works.

Computer-Managed Instruction

One of the most important potential uses of computers in schools is to individualize the educational process, a program referred to as Computer-Managed Instruction (CMI). In CMI, the primary function of the computer is to assist the teacher and student in teaching sequences where the actual instruction consists of programmed texts, taped lectures, prepared slides, and movies as well as textbooks and conventional classroom instruction.

A CMI system has the following as its objectives:

1. The collection and processing of student information (student's background and interests, his learning record and past educational achievements, and the like).
2. Instructional information (instructional means available for teaching certain topics).

3. The supplying of this information to the teacher in summarized form so that it can be used to best help the student. In this process, the computer is used to guide the student, at his choice and pace, through a planned series of alternative learning experiences.

Suppose that a history teacher wanted to teach a unit on the Civil War. She might say to her class, "Go to the Computer Library Center and dial 1-4-3-2-6 to begin your study of the Civil War." The computer would inform each student that he has three alternative choices in exploring the first unit of study:

1. To check out a taped lecture on the Civil War and listen to it in a carrel.
2. To look at a set of prepared slides with accompanying text.
3. To check out a programmed text.

The student has the option of using one or all of these materials, and he can periodically test himself on his progress. The results of his progress are stored to be available to the teacher. The rest of the units associated with this topic are handled in a similar manner.

There is a close relationship between Computer-Assisted Instruction (CAI) and CMI since both use the computer to assist the learner. CAI uses it to present information on a student terminal (teletypewriter, CRT display, image projector, or the like), whereas CMI uses the terminal to *manage* the instruction. CMI systems are based on clearly specifying *behavioral objectives* (what we want the student to accomplish), using the computer to measure a student's individual performance based on these objectives, and then prescribing from an inventory of instructional resources material related to the objectives and the student's needs. It is highly probable that CMI can improve individualized education, but only when more is learned about adapting education to individual requirements will it truly succeed.

Educational Time-Sharing Systems

Time-sharing, which is discussed in Chap. 8, allows many students and teachers to communicate with the computer in a *conversational mode.* Time-sharing systems are popular with schools because of the ease of usage and economy in having many students share in the simultaneous use of a computer. Many handy programming languages, such as BASIC and FORTRAN, are available for these systems.

Time-sharing systems may be found in institutions of higher learning as well as in elementary and secondary schools. The educational use of time-sharing was started at Dartmouth College in 1966. Since then, many universities and colleges have implemented systems to accommodate not only their own students but also nearby schools.

Educational time-sharing services are also made available to schools by commercial time-sharing service companies. Although the costs associated with

West Point cadets using CRT display terminals to communicate with the Point's time-sharing computer system. (*Courtesy*, United States Military Academy)

using commercial time-sharing services is often much lower than owning a comparable computer system, many schools have explored the use of low-cost, in-house time-sharing systems. These systems usually consist of a mini-computer (small, limited digital computer), a disk unit, several teletypewriters (usually up to 16), and an operating system. As with commercial service, users can communicate with these systems either through a teletypewriter or standard telephone lines.

Administrative Data Processing

Why should a teacher or school administrator be required to devote his much needed time and strength to such ordinary tasks as recording attendance, filling out grade reports, collecting grade cards, posting grades and test results for student records, scheduling students into classes, scoring and analyzing results of tests, conducting the scholastic census, constructing a master schedule of classes for students to be scheduled into, and the like?

Years ago teachers and administrators had no choice; they had to squeeze these chores into an already busy schedule. Today, however, the application of computer technology to these routines has freed many teachers and administrators from having to do them. The result: colleges and schools are improving the level of their services, teachers are devoting more time to *teaching*, administrators are spending more time with more critical problems, and school records are more accurate and appear without fuss in standardized formats.

Recommended Reading

Layman's Guide to the Use of Computers, Association for Educational Data Systems, Washington, D.C., 1971.

Computer-Assisted Instruction, A Book of Readings, Atkinson, R. C., and Wilson, H. A., eds., Academic Press, 1969.

Bushnell, D.D., and Allen, D.W., *The Computer in American Education*, Wiley, 1967.

Caffrey, J., and Mosmann, C.J., *Computers on Campus*, American Council on Education, Washington, D.C., 1967.

University Education in Computing Science, Finerman, A., ed., Academic Press, 1968.

Goodlad, J.I., O'Toole, Jr., J.F., and Tyler, L.L.,*Computers and Information Systems in Education*, Harcourt, Brace & World, 1966.

Hicks, B.L., and Honka, S., *The Teacher and the Computer*, W. B. Sanders Co., 1972.

Kaimann, R.A., and Marker, R.W., *Educational Data Processing: New Dimensions and Prospects*, Houghton Mifflin, 1967.

Margolin, J.B., and Misch, M.R., *Computers in the Classroom*, Spartan Books, 1970.

Martin, J., and Norman, A.R.D., *The Computerized Society*, Prentice-Hall, 1970, Chaps. 6 and 23.

Computer-Assisted Instruction and the Teaching of Mathematics, National Council of Teachers of Mathematics, Washington, D. C., 1969.

Oettinger, A., *Run, Computer, Run*, Harvard University Press, 1969.

Post, D.D., *The Use of Computers in Secondary School Mathematics*, Entelek Inc., Newburyport, Mass., 1970.

Spencer, D.D., *A Guide to Teaching About Computers in Secondary Schools*, Abacus Computer Corp., Ormond Beach, Fla., 1973.

8

Computers in Business

Soon after the potential of the computer became clear, American business became its biggest booster since it was faced with an ever-increasing paper-work explosion. It is estimated that over 20 percent of the total output of goods and services in the U.S. is devoted to reports, statistical information, billing, payroll, and other paper work. The computer has helped businessmen improve control over the billing of customers, calculating workers' pay and taxes, updating inventories, forecasting markets, and controlling a host of other administrative functions. Over half the computers in the United States are used by business to control and reduce administrative paper work and costs. Let us look at some typical business scenes today, running the gamut from small to large, showing how business has computerized itself.

Banking

The banking industry has seen many changes since the "Bank Holiday" of 1933. These changes have created the so-called "banking revolution." The computer, while not the cause of this revolution, definitely helped accelerate it. The revolution caused a "paper explosion." The volume of checks cleared by the banking system has increased over 1,100 percent in the past three decades. The computer has enabled the banks to process this great flood of paper rapidly and at a reasonable cost. Checks are now automatically processed and credited to or drawn against individual banks or accounts all over the country in a time span measurable in hours rather than in days or weeks, as had been the case. Only computer systems make it economically possible to process millions of items a day as is necessary in many large banks. The use of the computer for day-to-day processing of customer accounts and the processing and clearing of checks is now routine in all larger banks throughout the country.

Several banks are developing a voice answer-back system, in which a teller uses a special phone to dial the computer and receive the information needed to respond to a customer's request from a file of prerecorded spoken words under

Bank computer terminal records deposits and withdrawals and enters interest on passbook while updating master record of the account stored in computer storage. (*Courtesy,* IBM Corp.)

computer control. Such a system tied in to a completely automated central file would be invaluable to bank management.

Wall Street

An unprecedented volume of trading characterizes today's stock market. Inevitably, paperwork problems have proportionately increased. In some cases trading has had to stop just to allow stock market brokers to keep up. The Securities and Exchange Commission requires all brokerage houses to figure and post every transaction of the day before they may open for business the following day. Computers are used by large brokerage houses to handle literally millions of accounts. Not only can they perform the bookkeeping much faster but they can also achieve far greater accuracy than that attainable with previous accounting methods.

Check processing, account updating, and lean accounting can all be accomplished at the same time with data-processing systems such as the NCR Century 300. (*Courtesy,* National Cash Register Co.)

The New York Stock Exchange uses a computer-based system to speed the trading of information from the floor of the Exchange. The system uses optical data "readers" to read ordinary pencil-marked cards that report sales and quotations. Official reporters of the Exchange jot on a card the details of a sale—the kind of stock, its price, and the number of shares traded. The card is inserted into the reader, and the computer causes the information to be transmitted to 9,000 Exchange tickers and display boards around the world.

Insurance

Two decades ago, the State Farm Mutual Automobile Insurance Company actually used messengers on roller skates in an effort to speed internal communications and keep up with the mounting flow of paperwork. Today, State Farm, as well as most other insurance companies, uses computers to handle in minutes transactions that used to take days to process.

Next to the Federal Government, insurance companies are probably the second largest users of computers. The Metropolitan Life Insurance Company, in the mid 1950's, became the first insurance company to seek their aid. Virtually all insurance companies have now followed their pioneering path. In addition to performing the administrative work associated with customer policies, computers are used to prepare actuarial tables and devise plans suitable for particular classes of insurance.

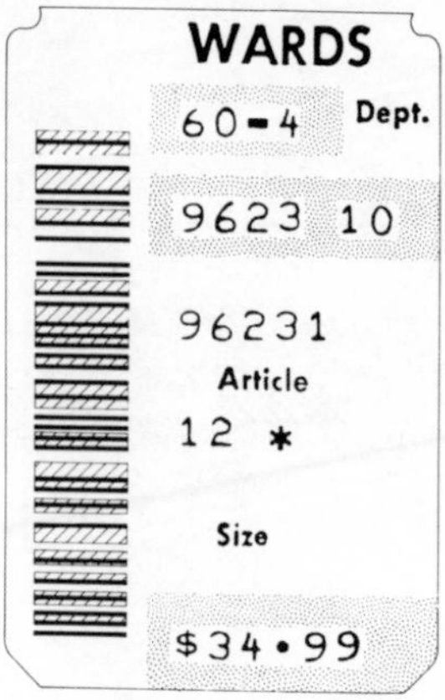

WARDS

60 ▬ 4   Dept.

96 23   10

96231

Article

12 *

Size

$34•99

Merchandise tag to be scanned by a wand reader.

Inventory Control

Last year, while the author was driving through northwest Washington with his family, one of his children wanted a Royalburger. The family stopped at the next Jr. Hot Shoppe to order one. The girl at the checkout register punched a key marked RBG and out popped the change: 55 cents. Her punching automatically sent a series of electronic impulses (over common telephone wires) to a computer system four miles away. The next morning, the computer added the number of Royalburger patties sold the day before in all the Jr. Hot Shoppes. It subtracted that number from the number of patties in the supply center. It compared the result with the number of patties estimated to be needed that day, and printed an order for the right number of patties to be brought to the center. The computer also printed a list of how many patties and buns were to be trucked to each Shoppe.

Computers are being used in many similar applications wherever vast numbers of items are either bought, stored, or sold. The computer is rapidly changing the internal operations of department stores, supermarkets, retail food outlets, warehouses, and countless other businesses requiring automated inventory control.

Most department store computer systems start at the "point-of-sale" with information generated by cash register tapes. As the sales person rings up the purchase, the tape is imprinted with a series of specially designed numbers containing the item code, the purchase price, the customer's account number for charge sales, and the identification code of the sales person.

When the tape has been completely filled, or at the end of the sales day, it is removed and read by an optical reader that transmits the information directly into computer storage. Using this information, the computer prepares a report of the day's sales by item, department, and total store. The computer updates the store's inventory and advises management of any items that must be reordered. At the same time, customer charge accounts are debited, and the payroll records of the sales personnel are credited for commission purposes.

In many department and clothing stores whenever you buy, say, a dress, the salesgirl will tear off a portion of the price ticket that contains a set of holes. Such stubs are used to supply information to the computer. With this data, the computer can produce reports showing what dress styles are selling best and thus facilitate reordering.

In another system, the merchandise tag is not removed from the article. Rather, it is automatically scanned by a hand-held wand reader for price and identification. After the customer's bill is computed, this data is then sent to a computer system where it helps produce an accurate picture of sales.

One interesting computer-controlled warehouse system was designed by Aerojet-General. The system employs a computer to control a "robot warehouseman" that can lift palletized 3000-pound loads from 60-foot-tall storage racks as well as to prepare printed transaction details for inventory control and invoicing. The computer can instruct the crane to store, retrieve, store and retrieve, move a load from one location to another, and so forth. This heavy-duty system can be easily operated by a secretary. Working from a shipment's lading bills, the secretary has only to feed descriptive information into the computer via a teletypewriter. From this point on, the computer takes command. The crane glides through the warehouse under complete control of the computer.

Computerized Supermarkets

Today, not many supermarkets are using computers in store checkout areas. In years to come, however, computerized supermarkets may become rather commonplace. One Food Fair Store in California is already using a computerized checkout system. How does it work? At first glance the store appears to be like all other supermarkets. However it is actually divided into seven departments, each having items marked with its own color-code number: blue labels for groceries, red for meat, and so on. Odd-weight cuts of meat and unpackaged vegetables and fruits have no price stamped on them, only a posted price per pound.

The checker uses a special cash register, called a counter terminal, to enter purchases. Its keyboard has quantity keys, item code keys, and department keys color-coded to match the colored labels on food items. When the checker presses a key, a display panel on the counter terminal flashes the correct price. The checker never has to look up multiple price breaks, worry about mix and match sales, check daily price changes, memorize limited-period sales prices, refund cash for coupons or return of bottles, or compute trading stamp and tax totals. When odd-weight items are placed on a scale next to the terminal, the correct

Automatic warehouse system controlled by a secretary and a computer. (*Courtesy*, Varian Associates)

price automatically appears on a display unit and is printed on the customer's tape receipt. The computer does it all—even to notifying the checker by light display if an invalid entry has been made.

The customer has an accurate, detailed record, including departmental and item code number information, on his receipt tape. And the checker, spared from mental gymnastics, has extra moments to give the customer more personal attention. But perhaps the most valuable asset of the system is its capability for almost instantaneously updating inventory records. This allows for more accurate ordering. When the checker records an item purchased (or returned), the store inventory of the item is automatically corrected.

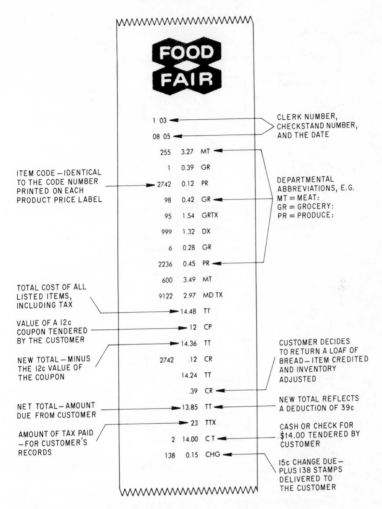

Customer's tape of a purchase includes item codes with associated price and department. (*Courtesy,* Honeywell)

The store manager has a terminal which he can use to check his inventory of any product, to determine sales up to the moment in any department or at any checkstand, to know total sales, to change prices, and the like. The system allows him to avoid both shortages and over-stocking. In addition, his books are balanced more accurately because precise computer prices have replaced checker arithmetic.

A daily sales report showing the number of customers handled by each checker at each checkstand enables management to schedule and rate store personnel. Another daily sales report tabulated by department permits management to evaluate such factors as general store operation and effectiveness of

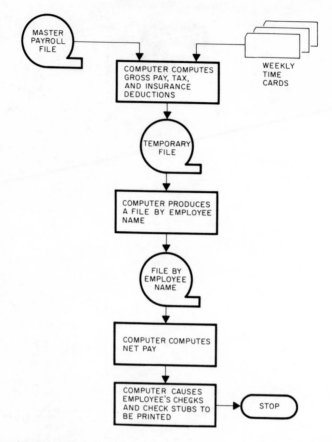

Pictorial description of how a computer is used in processing a payroll application.

special promotions. Other reports include daily invoices and receipts, weekly sales reports, weekly reports of low-turnover products, and weekly stockkeeping reports.

Payroll

Payment of employees is one of the most important areas of any business. Computers are used to process payroll in all large corporations and in many businesses with as few as 50 employees. A computerized payroll system performs the following computations:

- Regular earnings
- Overtime earnings
- Federal Income Tax withholdings

- State Income Tax withholdings
- City Income Tax withholdings
- Social Security withholdings
- Union dues
- Insurance deductions
- Miscellaneous deductions
- Gross earnings
- Net pay
- Year-to-date quantities

The following example will illustrate how a computer is used to process a payroll. The hours worked for each employee are first recorded on punched cards. A master file of previous employee payroll information is contained on magnetic tape. Both the magnetic tape and the punched cards are entered into the computer. The computer computes the gross pay and tax and insurance deductions for each employee and records this information on a temporary file. This file, which is ordered by employee identification number, is used to produce a file ordered by employee name. The computer uses the latter file to compute the employee's net pay and produces checks and listings of each employee's name and net pay.

Government

The United States government is the largest user of computers. Increases in population, more complex tax laws, and the increasing role of government have made them indispensable. Not only has the government been a leader in adopting computer processing techniques to its ever growing volume of work, it also financed the development of practically all early computers.

The Veterans Administration and the Department of Agriculture were among the first organizations to use computers for record keeping, payroll, and centralized accounting. The Census Bureau uses computers to determine the population census. By now, insurance systems such as Medicare, veteran insurance benefits, federal government retirement plans, and social security are heavily computer controlled.

The Internal Revenue Service uses computers to check and control income tax collection. Information on tax returns, sent to regional IRS centers, is first recorded on punched cards and then fed into computers. The computer checks the mathematical accuracy of the returns and makes preliminary calculations on tax deductions and exemptions. If the return contains a mistake, the computer causes correction notices to be printed. Correct returns are transferred to magnetic tape. These tapes are then forwarded to the IRS center in Martinsburg, West Virginia. At this center a computer system checks each return against all reports of payments to that individual or business from all sources, such as dividends from stocks, wages, interest from banks, and the like. If the return is not within standard guidelines, the computer prints a message indicating that it requires further checking by an IRS representative.

The use of computers by the IRS has increased collections and reduced tax evasion and delinquencies. It is expected that by 1980, the volume of tax returns will be approximately 137 million, a massive amount of information indeed. To eliminate some of the paper documents involved, the IRS is now accepting magnetic tapes from industry containing reports of wages, interest, and dividend payments. Someday, perhaps, industry's computers will communicate directly with IRS computers.

An Aid to Management

Computers have brought about important changes in the techniques of management by putting executives into closer contact with activities under their control. Facts are now immediately available to help them make decisions and give instructions to their subordinates.

Management is usually divided into three categories: top, middle, and lower management. Each level is interested in different types of information. Lower management must be provided with all facts essential to their activities: awareness of employee activities, availability of materials, work flow, and like details. Middle management is more interested in the progress of work under its control. Top management is interested in summarized reports and analyses free

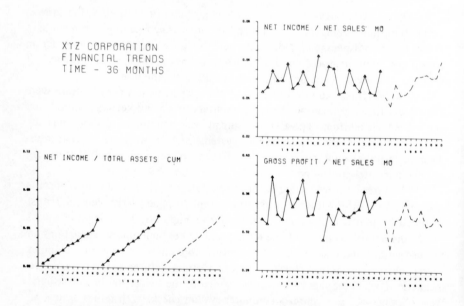

Computer-produced financial trend charts for helping business executives make decisions. (*Courtesy*, California Computer Products Inc.)

SOLD TO	SHIP TO	INVOICE NO.	PAGE

SPERRY RAND
315 PARK AVE SO
NEW YORK   10 N Y

SANDS AND CO.
260 09 57 AVENUE
NEW YORK   62 N Y

INVOICE NO. A21259   PAGE 1
INVOICE DATE 10 29 62
CUST. ORDER NO 10023

TERMS   2% 10 DAYS   SHIP VIA BEST WAY

ORIGINAL INVOICE

STOCK NUMBER	DESCRIPTION	QUANTITY ORDER	SHIP	B O	UNIT PRICE	SUGGESTED RET. PRICE	AMOUNT
850	TEAPOT	4	4		4.00	6.00	16.00
850A	TEAPOT LID	4	4		2.00	2.80	8.00
852	WATER PITCHER	1	1		4.00	6.00	4.00
101	16 PC STARTER SET	1	1		22.50	29.95	22.50
903	DINNER PLATE	12	12		1.25	1.75	15.00
905	SALAD PLATE	6	6		1.00	1.50	6.00
	PATTERN NO. 326	28*	28*				71.50*
853	MILK PITCHER	8	8		3.00	4.35	24.00
	PATTERN NO. 459	8*	8*				24.00*
859	COFFEE POT	2	2		4.50	6.75	9.00
859A	COFFEE POT LID	2	2		.75	1.10	1.50
861	CASSEROLE	4	4		6.00	9.00	24.00
963	ASHTRAY	6	6		.95	1.35	5.70
955	MUG	7	7		1.30	1.95	9.10
	PATTERN NO. 460	21*	21*				49.30*

BAL FWD   144.80

- FULL 132 CHARACTER PRINT LINE
- 2 PART FORM–INVOICE AND SHIPPING ORDER
- 300-400 LINE PER MINUTE PRINTING
- COMPUTED EXTENSIONS - UNIT PRICE X QUANTITY = AMOUNT
- UNIT WEIGHT X QUANTITY = GROSS WEIGHT

U3896C   PRINTED IN U.S.A.

Computer-prepared billing and shipping form. (*Courtesy,* Univac Division, Sperry Rand Corp.)

of the details needed by middle management. Care must be taken to avoid sending each level inappropriate data. This is a proper job for the computer. It can sift out useless facts and present important ones understandably.

Most computer systems in business offices process payroll, routine statistics, and accounting. Such systems have essentially automated routine clerical work. Several businesses have gone another step and implemented systems that provide centralized control over stocks, business forecasts, and financial reports.

A computer system in the Chemical Division of General Mills enables it to improve customer service by reducing order turn-around time from two days to the same day, prepare invoices within 24 hours instead of two to three days after shipments, exercise better control over accounts receivable, and produce more comprehensive and detailed sales and margin reports. At the same time, its data base provides a centralized source of market information for planning purposes.

Management Information Systems (MIS) are being developed by several businesses to provide executives with up-to-the-minute information about company operations and, when required, to aid in decision making. Ideally, for this to occur, the entire business would have to be simulated as well as the area in

Executive using management information presented on a display terminal.
(*Courtesy*, Control Data Corp.)

which it operates—a capability presently beyond the scope of modern mathematical and computer techniques. It is certainly feasible, however, for an MIS system to produce reports describing past activities of the company. A somewhat more advanced MIS could offer some capability of projecting trends and analyzing important facets of the company's business.

Business Planning

Detailed planning for the accomplishment of set objectives is an essential feature of effective management. Planning establishes exactly how and when various activities which are part of a long-run program will be carried out. It forecasts the needs for men and materials and devises ways to make the best use of all resources.

Thorough planning can more than pay for the effort it requires. Projects scheduled to make the best use of manpower will result in an even work load, avoiding periods of idleness as well as last minute subcontracting or hiring of new employees. Proper planning prevents both the over- and under-purchasing of equipment or supplies needed, and by avoiding last minute buying, it can obtain the best possible purchase price.

Effective planning, however, is not easily accomplished. Consider the problem of plotting out a year's activity for a construction firm employing some 1,000 people with varying skills and involved in more than 100 different projects. Such a large number of variables must be considered that it is quite difficult to decide just how to begin. Once an approach is decided upon, there still remains an almost unlimited number of possible plans. How is the planner to choose?

Fortunately, computers can help planners produce optimized schedules. Let us suppose that a large engineering consulting firm is interested in improving its planning. Their primary resource is their employees: approximately 2,000 engineers with backgrounds in mechanical, electrical, civil, and industrial engineering, supplemented by a large number of draftsmen and designers. The firm specializes in the design and construction of complex facilities like dams, bridges, and power plants.

The firm must schedule some 14 simultaneous projects. A number of these projects, although different in detail, require the same kind of personnel. The problem is to determine how to allocate manpower without violating deadlines. Data describing the projects (such as earliest start date, latest completion date, intermediate milestones, and so forth) are used as input to a computer and a previously prepared scheduling program. The computer then processes this data and generates reports that identify potential bottlenecks, shortages of resources and periods of idleness. With this information, the engineering firm can expect to achieve an optimal allocation of personnel.

A computer miles away records a book loan transaction at this input terminal of a library network. Book and borrower identification, other information, or queries are sent using the keyboard unit at the rear. Computer responses are received in typewritten form. In the foreground is a card-reading unit for processing book cards.

Information Retrieval

Computerized information storage and retrieval systems are capable of storing vast amounts of data in a centralized data bank that can be accessed by users located miles away. The fields of medicine, law, and scientific research, government agencies, libraries, and other organizations that are repositories of information are potential users of such systems (see page 119).

The medical field, in particular, seems ripe for a data bank that could be simultaneously shared by doctors, hospitals, public health officials, and researchers. Imagine a medical information system that stores the case histories of millions of patients and make this data available in a matter of seconds to any

```
THE INADEQUACY OF THE        ALPHABETICAL SUBJECT INDEX.              POLLAF-   -IAS
   CORRELATIVE INDEXES 1.     ALPHEBETICAL CORRELATIVE INDEXES.       BERNC  -56-CI1
                             AMBIGUITY OF SYNTACTIC FUNCTION RESO     KOUTA  -57-ASF
                THE          AMERICAN BAR FOUNDATION PROJECT ON T     MACK   -57-ABF
   E INFORMATION CENTER OF    AMERICAN CYNAMID-S STAMFORD LABORATO    FUNKCE-57-ICA
            INTRODUCING       AMERICAN DOCUMENTATION.                 TATEVD-   -IAD
OCUMENTARY REPRODUCTION       AMERICAN HISTORICAL ASSOCIATION.        CRLIB -53-GPC
ION-GATHERING HABITS OF       AMERICAN MEDICAL SCIENTISTS.            HERNS -   -IHA
       SOME NOTES ON          AMERICAN PRACTICE IN DOCUMENTATION.     COBLH  -50-SNA
OCEEDINGS CONFERENCE OF       AMERICAN SCIENTIFIC AND TECHNICAL AB    CONFAS-   -PCA
SOURCES- A CHALLENGE TO       AMERICAN SCIENCE AND INDUSTRYo         SHERJH-58-IRC
ROJECT ON THE SURVEY OF       AMERICAN STATUTORY LAW.                 MACK   -57-ABF
YAL TROPICAL INSTITUTE,       AMSTERDAM-NETHERLANDS.                  HECKFP-55-DBT
   A METHOD OF KEEPING        ANAESTHESIA RECORDS AND ASSESSING RE    NOSWOR-43-MKA
IBM 990 SPECIAL INDEX         ANALYZER.                               MURPRW-58-I9S
CORDING OF SURGICAL AND       ANESTHETIC DATA IN MILITARY SERVICE.    WANGCP-41-ERS
TION IN THE LIBRARY- AN       ANNOTATED BIBLIOGRAPHY.                 KENTA -56-ALA
                 AN          ANTIBIOTIC LITERATURE FILE FOR CHEMI    OHRMME-54-ALF
            USE OF           APERTURE CARDS FOR THE CONSOLIDATION    SLATPM-58-UAC
ENT AND PROOF SERVICES.       APG.                                    KENTP -53-TIU
E DATA HANDLING SYSTEM.       APPENDIX A. MACHINE TRANSLATING OF L    RAMOWC-57-DSI
IONS, WITH REFERENCE TO       ARCHAEOLOGICAL DOCUMENTS.               GARDJC-  -CGS
ANIZATION AND STATUS OF       ARCHIVAL TRAINING IN THE UNITED STAT    TREVKL-48-OSA
          ABSTRACT           ARCHIVE OF ALCOHOL LITERATURE.          JELLEM-48-AAA
       THE NATIONAL          ARCHIVES.                                BAHMRH-55-NAA
       SCIENTIFIC FILM       ARCHIVES.                                MICHAR-55-SFA
TERIAL IN LIBRARIES AND       ARCHIVES.                              UNESCO-56-MML
                             ARCTIC BIBLIOGRAPHY.                     TREMM -55-AB
                THE          ARMED FORCES MEDICAL LIBRARY.* ITS S     USARFM-54-AFM
                             ARMED SERVICES TECHNICAL INFORMATION     BARDWA-56-AST
                THE          ARMY MEDICAL LIBRARY RESEARCH PROJEC     LARKSV-49-AML
METHODS USED BY THE U S       ARMY ORDNANCE CORP IN DEPOT OPERATIO    ALLOAJ-  -IRM
       DOCUMENTATION AT       ASCONA.                                 REV DO-50-DA
DOCUMENTATION IN SOUTH        ASIA.* PRO SPEED AND COVERAGE.          SHEEP -  -RTS
IN SOUTH AND SOUTH EAST       ASIAN COUNTRIES.* TOUR REPORT.          SHIEP -56-SID
                             ASM-SLA METALLURGICAL LITERATURE CLA     MAIEAT-  -AML
       ADAPTATION OF         ASM-SLA METALLURGICAL LITERATURE CLA     WEILBH-57-AAM
         REVISION OF         ASM-SLA METALLURGICAL LITERATURE CLAS    FOSTLS-58-RAM
CAL REPORTS IN MULTIPLE       ASPECT SEARCHING FOR INFORMATION RET    WHALFR-57-DII
            MULTIPLE         ASPECT SEARCHING FOR INFORMATION RET     ARMEST-57-MAS
       THE WORD             ASSOCIATION MATRIX.* A DEVICE TO RED     COLLCH-  -WAM
RMATION BY MEANS OF THE       ASSOCIATION OF IDEAS.                   TAUBM -55-SRI
UNITERM SYSTEM AND THE        ASSOCIATION OF IDEAS TO A SPECIAL LI    TAUBM -  -AUS
ON LOGICAL PRODUCTS AND       ASSOCIATIONS.                           TAUBM -55-SNL
   A MULTIDIMENSIONAL         ASSOCIATOR.                             BUSSG -57-MA
                             ASTIA ESTABLISHED TO INTEGRATE SCIEN     TECHUD-51-AE1
T AT THE LIBRARY OF THE       ATOMIC ENERGY RESEARCH ESTABLISHMENT    ASHTHD-52-PIE
                THE          ATOMIC ENERGY COMMISSION LIBRARY SYS     FRY BM-50-AEC
H OF THE UNITED KINGDOM       ATOMIC ENERGY AUTHORITY.                HOGGIH-  -SCI
    YOUR COLLECTION OF        ATOMIC ENERGY LITERATURE.               RANDGE-51-YCA
EQUIREMENTS OF USERS OF       ATOMIC ENERGY INFORMATION THROUGH TH    HERNS -  -DIR
                THE          ATOMIC ENERGY COMMISSION LIBRARY SYS     COLLRL-50-AEC
                             AUSTRALIAN LIBRARIES AND THEIR METHO     UNESBL-57-ALT
D KINGDOM ATOMIC ENERGY       AUTHORITY.                              HOGGIH-  -SCI
S.* AN ELECTRONIC BRAIN       AUTHORS A BOOK.                         HALLE -56-MME
           CORPORATE         AUTHORS AND THE CATALOGING OF OFFICI     RUYSY -57-CAC
            EDITORS,         AUTHORS AND ABSTRACTS.                   LEE MU-56-EAA
    AN EXPERIMENT IN         AUTO ABSTRACTING.                        IBM RC-58-EAA
                             AUTO ENCODING OF DOCUMENTS FOR INFOR     LUHNHP-58-AED
                             AUTOMATA AND INFORMATION.                FAIRR -52-AI
                             AUTOMATED SEARCHING SECOND STEP.         CHEMEN-57-ASS
   IBM CARD SYSTEM           AUTOMATES LIBRARY CHARGE OUT.            IBM LN-57-ICS
THE PREPARATION OF           AUTOMATIC ABSTRACTS ON THE 704 DATA      SAVATR-58-PAA
NES, DOCUMENTATION, AND       AUTOMATIC CODING.                       GOTTJ -57-MOA
ON STANDARDS ELECTRONIC       AUTOMATIC COMPUTER /SEAC/.              MARDEC-58-FAP
```

Page from a "permuted title index" prepared by a computer. (*Courtesy*, Bell Telephone Laboratories)

qualified subscriber. These histories would contain the medical record of every individual, the symptoms of every complaint, the physician's diagnosis, inoculations given, treatments tried and their effectiveness, side effects of drugs administered, and so forth. Every physician could use this vast store of information as a sort of electronic medical consultant to check and validate his own decisions and diagnosis.

In the field of law, large information banks of data could provide lawyers and court officials with a library of all laws, rulings, case histories, and procedures that are relevant to any particular need. A lawyer would be able to compress many man-years of tedious legal research and analysis activities into a few minutes of computer time.

The page from a "permuted title index" shown here was produced by a digital computer programmed to organize and list document titles alphabetically according to their important words. Each title appears in the index in as many places as it has significant words. Each significant word appears, in turn, at the index position.

Recommended Reading

Clark, J.O.E., *Computers At Work,* Grosset & Dunlap, 1971, pp. 101-112.
Gerald, C.F., *Computers and the Art of Computation,* Addison-Wesley, 1971, Chap. 12.
Martin, J., *The Computerized Society,* Prentice-Hall, 1970.
Spencer, D.D., *Introduction to Information Processing,* Charles E. Merrill, 1974.
Thomas, S., *Computers,* Holt, Rinehart and Winston, 1965.
Computer Usage: Applications, Weiss, E.A., ed., McGraw-Hill, 1970.

9

Computers for Control

We are all familiar with noncomputer control systems, such as the thermo-stat and valves that regulate a home air conditioning and heating system or the fuse that detonates a bomb at the point of impact. Simply speaking, control systems are systems that perform required operations when certain specific conditions occur. They relieve man of many monotonous, time-consuming chores. The computer has characteristics that make it highly useful as a control element for a control system. A few computer-controlled systems are described in this chapter.

Process Control Systems

Computer control of industrial processes is slightly over a decade old. Today computers are used for this purpose particularly in the following indus-tries:

- Utilities (for steam plant logging and control, substation logging, economic dispatch)
- Metal works (for blast furnaces, oxygen converters, reversing hot mills, hot strip mills, tandem cold mills)
- Chemical plants (for reaction, blending and mixing, distillation, purifica-tion)
- Cement plants (for raw materials blending, kiln control)
- Food processing (for mixing, blending, cooking, inventory)
- Manufacturing (for quality control, conveyor control, testing, checkout)
- Petroleum plants (for cracking, crude distillation, reforming, alkylation, blending)
- Paper mills (for paper machines, digesters, chemical recovery)

A computer will do whatever it can be instructed to do; in process control its most important functions are as follows:

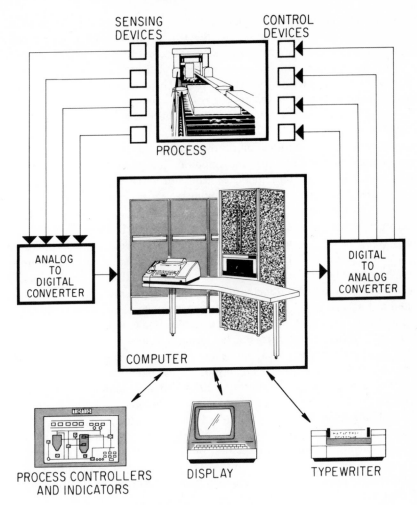

SENSING DEVICES

CONTROL DEVICES

PROCESS

ANALOG TO DIGITAL CONVERTER

DIGITAL TO ANALOG CONVERTER

COMPUTER

PROCESS CONTROLLERS AND INDICATORS

DISPLAY

TYPEWRITER

On-line computer control of a process.

- Maintaining product quality
- Watching for alarm conditions
- Logging performance data
- Presenting information to human operators in an easy-to-use format
- Maximizing output
- Maximizing profit for a given output

There are two basic types of process-control systems. In an *off-line computer-controlled system*, the computer does not itself control the plant; the process remains under the direct control of human operators. Readings from various sources of information, such as instruments measuring the input of raw materials, pressures, temperatures, and flows of the process variables, are taken at specified intervals, converted into digital form, and transmitted to a computer to calculate and type out (or otherwise display) figures indicating the state of the process for the benefit of the operators. The computer provides operating guides for the settings of all values—power inputs and the like.

In a *closed-loop computer-controlled system,* the computer is directly in charge of the process since it adjusts all controls from the information provided by sensing devices. If information on the state of the process is required, either continuously or intermittently, the computer can present this information as typed data, magnetic tape, punched cards, or on a CRT display. In many cases a computer can more nearly optimize the process than can a human operator, partly because the operator is rarely given, or rarely could absorb, enough information, and partly because optimization requires the solution of many complicated equations. Consider the following process-control application.

All of the automotive glass presently manufactured by the Ford Corporation is originally produced in a continuous one-eighth-inch thick sheet, 100 inches wide, by a computer-controlled float-glass process. This process, originated in England, takes its name from a step in the operation where molten glass is floated on a bath of molten tin. First, 300 to 400 tons per day of the raw materials, including feldspar, rouge, charcoal, cullet, soda ash, salt cake, dolomite, limestone, and sand, are heated in a natural gas furnace to a temperature of 2,900°F. The glass is homogenized, just like milk, by being cooled to 2,000°F, and is then poured onto the 175-foot bath of liquid tin. As the glass travels over the tin, its temperature is gradually lowered to 1,200°F. From the tin bath the glass goes into a 350-foot annealing (tempering) oven where a gradual reduction in temperature to 250°F equalizes its internal stresses and prevents blemishes. When the glass rolls out at the end of the line to be cut into sheets, it drops to room temperature. At this point the glass is finished. Grinding and polishing operations are not required since the glass has already taken on the perfect flatness of the molten tin.

The controlling computer handles approximately 500 analog signals and 200 digital signals 30 times each second. It uses 80 closed control loops to maintain correct conditions in the melting furnace, the tin bath (and its nitrogen atmosphere system), and the annealing oven (called a lehr). The signals originate at some 700 sensing devices located in the furnace, lehr, and other key points, and monitor variables such as temperature, level of molten glass, and liquid and gas flow. The computer compares each signal with a range table and if a variable goes out of bounds, either corrects it with one of its control loops or prints an alert for the human operators. With direct digital control of the process, critical temperatures in the 2,000°F range can be controlled to within one degree and pressures in the furnace can be held constant within two one-hundredths of an inch.

Programming a computer for process control differs from that for other purposes. Compared with scientific and business programs, process control programs have more instructions, more parallel paths, and more built-in safeguards. Once loaded into the computer, the programs remain undisturbed for long periods of time.

Military Defense Systems

The development of large-scale computer systems has been sponsored primarily by the federal government, and within the government, primarily for defense. The first computer, ENIAC, was developed to compute ballistic tables. Magnetic-core memory was first developed for the SAGE air-defense computer. Today, defense needs continue to stimulate developments for faster machines, larger storage facilities, and more reliable components.

In military command-and-control systems, computers are used to aid the human decision maker. They speed his responses and extend his span of control. Outstanding examples of command-and-control systems are SAGE, SPADATS, NTDS, and BMEWS. A short description of these systems follows.

SAGE SAGE (Semi-Automatic Ground Environment) is a computer-controlled air-defense system. It is the granddaddy of all large-scale command-and-control systems, combining surveillance with weapons control and providing a commander, instantly and continuously, with the information needed to run an air battle. Prior to the introduction of SAGE, air defense was essentially built around the "eyeball and grease pencil" methods of World War II.

SAGE combines the assets of radar, high-speed communications, and electronic computers to enormously reduce the time required for locating hostile aircraft and launching an attack. The computer assembles, stores, and evaluates data supplied from radar on the ground, at sea, and in the air; displays information on a screen with unnecessary data eliminated; and advises a commander of the best weapons to employ against approaching targets.

SAGE assimilates mountains of information on weather, status of weapons, flight plans of all air traffic, and radar observations. It compares radar inputs with known flight plans of friendly traffic in order to determine the presence of unknown craft. It then provides the information needed to intercept unfriendly targets at the most distant point as quickly as possible. Armed interceptors are dispatched to investigate, and further command decisions await the reports of their pilots.

SPADATS SPADATS (Space Detection and Tracking System) is an information-gathering system with the mission of tracking and keeping an up-to-date inventory of all objects in space orbit. The system involves a world-

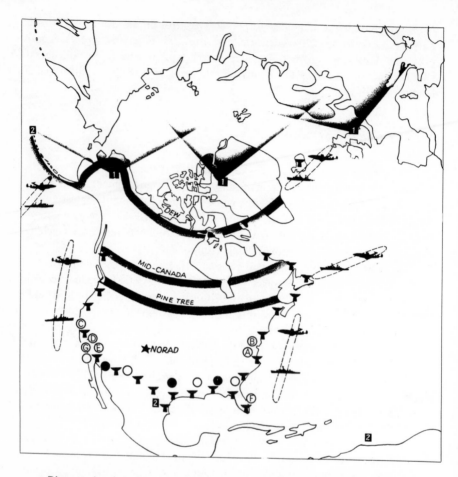

Diagram showing some of the stations involved in the North American Air Defense System (NORAD). (Key: A—SPASUR coordination center, Dahlgren, Va.; B—NASA's Goddard Space Flight Center; C—Discoverer tracking station; D—Edwards Air Force Base; E—NASA's Goldstone tracking and observation station; F—Atlantic Missile Range; G—Pacific Missile Range; 1—BMEWS stations; 2—USAF stations; •—SPASUR transmitters; ○—SPASUR receivers.

wide network of observation stations that report on their positions. A computer is used to help track, identify, and log these objects.

NTDS   NTDS (Naval Tactical Data System) is a command-and-control system for ships at sea. It uses computers, displays, radar video processors, data communication facilities, and other equipment to help make tactical decisions. Operationally, it (1) *coordinates* the collection of data from sources aboard ship (radar, sonar, navigation inputs, and so forth) and from external sources; (2) *correlates* this data to obtain a clear picture of the tactical situation; (3)

Computer-controlled display device used to present tactical information to military decision makers. (*Courtesy,* U.S. Air Force)

processes the data required for decision-making; and (4) *communicates* the decision for action to the appropriate weapons systems. Computers communicate with each other automatically via a data communication network and present tactical information via displays.

BMEWS   BMEWS (Ballistic Missile Early Warning System) uses three early-warning stations (in Thule, Greenland; Clear, Alaska; and Fylingdales Moor, Yorkshire, England). Information from these stations is expected to give a 15- to 20-minute warning of a missile attack and will be used to predict where the warheads will strike. Oriented generally northward toward the regions out of which Soviet missiles would rise, BMEWS radars can "see" for 3,000 miles with their 165 by 400 foot antennas. What they "see" and identify is sent to a network of computers that displays it for use by military decision makers.

Control of Machine Tools

Numerically controlled machines have taken on in recent years a large role in the war against climbing production costs. Perhaps the single most important advance in machining during the past decade, numerical control combines mass production capability with flexibility. Its machines can drill holes, stamp out parts, insert components, and perform numerous other operations with more reliability in a given time than human hands could ever achieve.

Shipboard computer system including a CP 642A computer, teletypewriter, and paper tape reader/punch. (*Courtesy,* U.S. Navy, Fleet Computer Programming Center)

By far the largest user of numerical control is the metal working industry, although there are other applications. The machining of metals requires only a small number of basic operations. Metal is cut by relative motion between the part and the cutter. Either the cutting tool above moves or both the tool and the part move. Most metal cutting can be called milling, but some types of cutting are common enough to have special-purpose machines. In general, a milling machine moves the part under a rotating cutter, and metal is removed from the outer and inner surfaces. The cutter can also gouge out holes of various geometrical dimensions. Other machines common to this industry are lathes, grinders, shapers, and drilling machines.

Numerical control offers economy because of its short runs for complex parts. It also reduces the need for special jigs and fixtures, shortens manufacturing lead times, decreases inventories, releases floorspace, and, in short, makes the entire manufacturing operation much more flexible.

Numerical control as applied to machine tools consists of the automatic control of all machine functions through a complete cycle by means of numerically coded instructions. Once a piece of work is placed in position on the machine, a coded program controls selection of the tools, feed rate, coolant

Milling machine directly controlled by a minicomputer. (*Courtesy,* Digital Equipment Corp.)

setting, spindle speed, and the direction and distance of cutting movements until the part is complete. Coded instructions to machine tools usually take the form of punched paper tape.

The procedure for producing a part on a numerical controlled tool is as follows:

1. The part to be produced is described in an easy-to-use numerical control language such as APT (Automatically Programmed Tool). This description is called a *part program.*

2. The part program is keypunched on cards, each card containing a specific machine tool instruction.

3. The computer accepts the part program and calculates the coordinate points that the machine tool will follow in producing the part.

4. The computer produces a punched paper tape.

5. The machine tool uses the paper tape to control its operations.

Most numerical controlled machine tools are controlled by paper tape, but in recent years, several machines have been developed that are controlled directly by the computer. The computer used in these systems is usually a minicomputer with few or no peripheral devices.

"That's the way the tape tore."

Recommended Reading

Clark, J.O.E., *Computers At Work,* Grosset & Dunlap, 1971, pp. 35-45, 113-119.

Favret, A.G., *Introduction to Digital Computer Applications,* Reinhold, 1965, Chap. 11.

Martin, J., and Norman, A.R.D., *The Computerized Society,* Prentice-Hall, 1970. Chap. 8.

Rothman, S., and Mosman, C., *Computers and Society,* Science Research Associates, 1972.

Sackman, H., *Computers, System Science, and Evolving Society,* Wiley, 1967.

10

Computers in Transportation

In the past decade, a whole new era of transportation has evolved. It was only a few years ago that man was first transported to outer space. Airlines have experienced extraordinary growth; passenger traffic has tripled, freight traffic is up five times, and mail volume is six times as great as it was a decade ago. Vehicular traffic is an increasing problem in all of our major cities. It is small wonder that the application of computers to transportation systems is becoming increasingly important. They launch and control space craft. They control air traffic at all major airports. Transportation reservations are often made using computerized reservation systems. City traffic is partially controlled in many cities by computer-controlled traffic lights. Ships are maneuvered across oceans under computer guidance. Let us now examine more closely how computers are used for these purposes.

Air Traffic Control

Air traffic is one of the fastest growing segments of the transportation business, with even greater growth promised by the introduction of larger and faster jet planes. To enable airway usage to keep pace with the sophistication of new aircraft, the airlines have supported efforts to modernize the airways and have publicly urged the Federal Aviation Agency (which has the major responsibility for controlling air traffic) to be more active toward that end.

The FAA is currently in the process of developing a computer-controlled air traffic system for major airports. It will eventually control take-offs, enroute flight, and landings, so as to relieve congestion at airports and provide accurate control of planes in flight to forestall collisions. Air traffic controllers now rely primarily on manual and visual methods of directing plane movements.

The world's busiest airport, O'Hare, in Chicago, handles some 30 million passengers a year; by 1980 the figure is expected to top 40 million. Over 1,600 flights per day are handled by its controllers. O'Hare airport uses a radar

Univac computer used to control air traffic at the world's busiest airport
(O'Hare, Chicago).

identification system called ARTS III. This system generates "beacon" signals to communicate with airborne electronic equipment in all aircraft within a 50-mile radius and receive basic information such as the identity of each aircraft, its altitude, and its speed. The data is processed by a computer and displayed graphically on a display device. Although the main objective of ARTS III is increased safety, it is expected that the system will eventually reduce airport delays because of the increased density of aircraft under its control.

Computerized Reservation Systems

Even though we entered the jet age about two decades ago, it has only been in recent years that the major airlines implemented computerized reservation systems. Without computers, it often took more time to get a confirmed reservation on a flight from Washington, D.C., to New York than it took to fly there. To retrieve the necessary information for booking such a flight, an airline ticket agent often had to thumb through two or three volumes the size of telephone books. He often used the back of an envelope to figure out the cost of the ticket, then wrote the ticket out by hand. Finally, when the passenger showed up at the airport, he sometimes discovered that some employee had goofed and sold him a seat on an airplane already fully booked or on a flight that had been cancelled. Such pencil and paper methods not only made air

American Airline agents taking bookings at desk-size consoles (top) are able to communicate instantaneously with computer center (bottom). In the foreground is the electronic unit where passenger information is stored. (*Courtesy,* American Airlines)

travelers unhappy but also caused many airline companies to lose money consistently.

To meet the growing demand for efficient reservations systems, the airlines turned to the computer. With the computer, airlines can make maximum use of every seat up to the moment of a plane's departure. Computer-controlled reservation systems provide airline clerks and travel agents with almost immediate access to up-to-the-minute information on space availability for all flights. When the reservation agent enters the proper numbers on a keyboard, she can instantly get a picture of the availability of all seats near the departure time requested. The information is either presented on a display screen or printed on the agent's terminal. As the reservations are entered into the system, the transactions are "edited" by the computer to insure that all necessary information has been included: the proper number of names for the seats reserved, home telephone numbers, auto rentals, hotel reservations, ticketing arrangements, or other special services.

If space is not available on a specific flight, the agent can advise the computer to put him on one or more waiting lists. When cancellations are received, the computer will automatically check these lists and notify the proper boarding city of the passenger entitled to the available space.

In addition to passenger reservations, most airline computer systems also process information on aircraft scheduling, airfreight and cargo loading, meal planning, personnel availability, and other similar functions.

One of the first computerized air reservation systems, called SABRE, was developed for American Airlines. SABRE handles all the mechanical functions and procedures associated with the sale, confirmation, and supervision of an airline reservation. Composed of two basic reservations records—passenger name and seat inventory—SABRE makes it possible for any of American's passengers to immediately confirm, alter, or cancel any or all of their itinerary no matter when or where the original reservation was made. In addition, the centralized computer system performs the following functions:

- Automatically notifies reservation agents when special action is required, such as calling a passenger to inform him of a change in flight status
- Maintains and quickly processes waiting lists of passengers desiring space on fully booked flights
- Sends messages to other airlines to request space and follows up if no reply is forthcoming
- Answers space requests from other airlines
- Provides arrival and departure times for all flights.

SABRE is capable of responding instantly to inquiries from anywhere in the network and storing ticket information for as long as 300 days into the future.

The nerve center of SABRE is a large computer system linked to about 2,000 outlets by more than 25,000 miles of communications lines. In a typical day, SABRE receives approximately 125,000 telephone calls. These include 60,000 requests for passenger reservations, 15,000 requests for space from other airlines, 8,000 inquiries for flight arrival and departure information, and 17,000 requests from other sources including American's own offices, travel agencies, and key accounts. The system that handles this tremendous work load is made up of three major elements—the agents' sets, the electronic reservations center, and the communications network.

A desk-size electronic console, outfitted with buttons, display lights and a keyboard much like that of a typewriter, the agent set gives the agent direct communication with the center. The computer's response to the agent's request for reservations is nearly instantaneous. And if data has been omitted, SABRE notifies the agent of the oversight. When the transaction is finished, the computer gives the agent a printed "OK" message, then stores the passenger record—including flight details—in its memory bank.

Computer-based reservation systems have also been developed for theatre and stadium seats, hotel accommodations, and auto rentals. One hotel reservation system in New York handles several thousand reservations per day. Agents enter the travelers' requirements into the system via display/keyboard terminals. The information is transmitted over telephone lines to a computer center. If the requested hotel is filled, alternatives are selected by the computer. Otherwise, the computer flashes "CONFIRMED" to the display terminal. This operation takes place in seconds.

Automated Passenger Processing

Airline terminals are becoming alarmingly crowded with passengers, a situation that will undoubtedly get worse as jet airplanes become larger and more people use air travel as a mode of transportation. Systems must be conceived and implemented to handle passenger flow on the ground. Anticipating passenger processing problems, several airlines and airline associations have adopted standards for magnetically encoded credit cards and tickets.

American Airlines was the first to introduce a passenger-operated automatic ticket vendor (ATV). Two ATV's, linked to a nearby computer, were installed at the American Airlines ticket counter at Chicago's O'Hare Airport. Each ticket vendor accepted magnetically encoded credit cards. Passengers using these self-service machines purchased tickets without the aid of airline personnel. The major goal of this system was to speed passengers through the airport.

Computers are used in airport terminals to control air traffic, to keep track of passenger seats, to control freight loading and unloading, to operate push-button ticketing systems, and to keep track of passenger luggage. Computers are also used to pinpoint the location of every plane in an airline's fleet and to report on its status and all the factors that affect its utilization.

If a passenger has made a reservation with American Airlines, he has only to insert his credit card into the ATV and press the "yes" button next to the question, "Do you have a reservation?" When he removes the credit card at the ATV's request, he receives his ticket within a few seconds. A passenger without a reservation can use the ATV to reserve either a first-class or coach accommodation on the next available flight to any of the following eleven destinations:

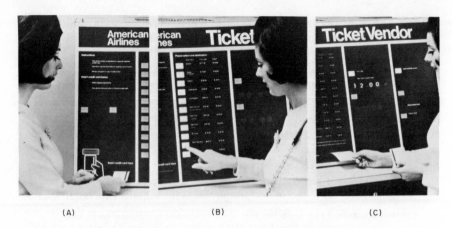

(A)   (B)   (C)

Computer-controlled ticket vendor allows passengers to purchase tickets on
their own by inserting a magnetically encoded credit card (a), choosing
destination (b), and receiving ticket (c), all in less than a minute. (*Courtesy,*
American Airlines)

Boston; Dallas-Fort Worth; Detroit; Indianapolis; Los Angeles; New York-
LaGuardia; New York-Newark; New York (no airport preference); St. Louis; San
Francisco; and Washington, D.C. Tickets are not issued until the passenger
retrieves his credit card in order to ensure that it is not left behind.

A second do-it-yourself ticketing system has been developed by American
Airlines and installed at airports in Boston, Washington, D.C., and New York.
This system, called JETS (Jet Express Ticketing System), permits passengers to
issue their own tickets and boarding passes. Utilizing a minicomputer and
American's central computer system, JETS processes each passenger in less than
eight seconds. Its ticketing machines are activated by special credit cards.
Passengers with reservations are issued tickets and boarding passes while those
without reservations must first push a button to choose between first class and
coach seating. JETS prints billing information in both cases.

Controlling Traffic

You pull up to a red light late at night. You wait. There are no cars in
sight, in any direction, but you wait. Finally, you are allowed to proceed until
you reach the next light, which is also red and still no other cars in sight. You
are the victim of a traffic controller, a small machine with clocks and cams
which controls the traffic signal lights.

There are several ways to solve your problem: you can run the red light
and get caught by the local constabulary, you can start riding a bicycle, you can
cry a lot, you can simply stay home, or you can move to one of the following
cities: New York City; San Jose, Calif.; Wichita Falls, Tex.; Fort Wayne, Ind.;

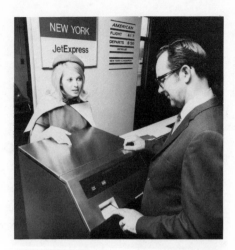

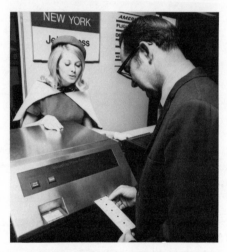

Having activated the JETS computer-controlled terminal with a credit card (top), passenger without reservation chooses first class rather than coach seating and receives ticket and boarding pass (bottom). (*Courtesy,* American Airlines)

Charleston, S.C.; or Baltimore, Md. Each of these cities (plus many more) uses a computerized traffic control system to help prevent this sort of thing from happening.

Today, most urban traffic is controlled by what are known as *open-loop* systems. These adjust signal settings at individual intersections as traffic conditions change. But since there is no provision for feedback of information to some control center monitoring an entire network, traffic may be kept moving well at one intersection only to jam up further down the line.

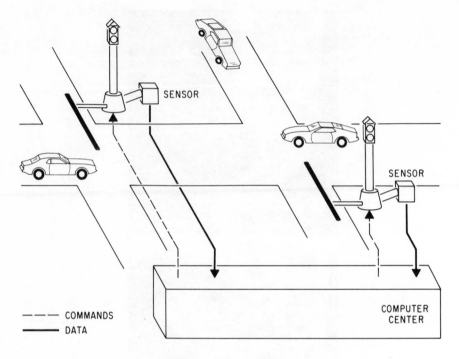

Sensors for monitoring traffic patterns.

The alternative is the *closed-loop* traffic control system. It links together in a monitoring-control network all intersections throughout an entire area. Because it has this overview, it can adjust individual local conditions to optimize the efficiency of the network as a whole. It operates in the following manner:

1. Traffic patterns and densities are "sensed" at each intersection on a continuous basis.
2. This data is communicated to a control center in effective real-time.
3. The center analyzes the data and makes an instant decision about the acceptability of the current situation.
4. If the situation is unacceptable, the center calculates what changes in signal settings (or other control devices) are necessary to improve it.
5. Appropriate implementation commands are sent to the individual signals and the monitoring phase repeated.

Control of any complex process demands information feedback on an almost instantaneous basis. In the closed-loop traffic system, vehicle "sensors" are used to determine when cars have passed a certain point, whether one or more is present in a specified area, and how fast they are passing through it. This information is then reported to the computer for analysis of traffic patterns at large.

"Sorry I'm late, Chief, but you've just no idea what the traffic's like this morning."

©DATAMATION

Real-time control of traffic signals by a computer first took place in Toronto, Canada in 1960. Since then many cities in the United States and Europe have followed suit. The first two systems in this country (San Jose and Wichita Falls) used IBM 1800 computers. The San Jose system controls 59 intersections and uses 400 detectors. The Wichita Falls system controls 57 intersections. European cities that have installed systems include Berlin, Vienna, Munich, Madrid, Barcelona, London, and Helsinki. The world's largest system is currently being installed in New York City, which has already automated over 500 intersections. Eventually, 7,500 of the city's 9000 intersections will be computer-controlled.

Computers are also being used to police freeway traffic. In Massachusetts, computer-controlled bands of light guide motorists onto Route 128 at an

Traffic monitoring system for John Lodge Freeway in Detroit.

entrance ramp. A railing on the left side of the ramp sparkles with bright green lights when it is safe to enter the expressway. The lights are controlled by near-by computers that receive messages from magnetic wire-sending loops buried in the expressway pavement. The lights are advisory only, and a driver may ignore them and find his own opening.

Traffic control systems are complex and therefore subject to many problems. Numerous delays have been encountered while installing the New York City system, although its successes have been encouraging. Officials in San Jose claim that traffic has been speeded. Wichita Falls reports a 9 percent drop in accidents and a 45 percent drop in the time spent waiting at red lights.

Some cities (Houston, Detroit, and Chicago) use closed-circuit television and a computer to reduce traffic jams. Sensing devices located at intervals along freeways detect gaps in traffic during peak hours. When one is detected, the computer turns an on-ramp traffic light green so that motorists can reach the freeway at the right time to enter the gap.

Rapid Transit Systems

Computers are used to control new urban rail transit systems such as the BART (Bay Area Rapid Transit) system in the San Francisco Bay area (which

BART subway train control system displays train operations on CRT console and display board above. A keyboard is used to request various displays. (*Courtesy,* Westinghouse Electric Co.)

opened about one-third of its trackage in the fall of 1972). The BART system is the first in the world to be completely automated. Along the 75 miles of tracks, including a stretch running below the Bay, will be 34 passenger stations in a three-county area. As many as 105 trains will be in operation during peak hours, some running as close as 90 seconds apart. The 72-passenger cars, assembled in trains up to 10 cars long, operate at maximum speeds of 80 mph. Including 20-second station stops, average speeds reach 50 mph. The computer system coordinates all trains and schedules and monitors their speeds. The human operator on each train does no "driving" at all unless the computer system fails, in which case he can intervene and drive the train at a top speed of 20 mph until the corrected system takes over again.

Computer-Directed Railroads

One of the major problems railroads share is the idle railroad freight car. For every working day, the average car curls up at customers' sidings three days and spends additional time in freight yards where cars are assembled into trains. The classification yard, that part of the freight yard where complete trains are broken up and reassembled, represents one of the biggest efficiency drains of all.

This bottleneck is being solved by using computers. The computer stores in its memory a list of what cars to shunt and where. After yard engines have pushed them up the far side of the hump (an incline that feeds cars onto the proper tracks for assembly into trains), the computer activates the proper switches, then brakes the cars for safe link-up.

Railroads in this country and Canada are also increasingly adopting the computerized ACI (Automated Car Identification) system to improve the control of freight cars. The system's sensing beams read a moving freight car's color-coded identification label to provide status and location information.

Shipboard Computers

For the past decade computers have been used aboard U. S. Navy vessels to track hostile aircraft, ships, and submarines and to help in their own defense at sea. Until recently, however, the use of computers aboard merchant and passenger ships has been limited.

Several major disasters in the English Channel and San Francisco Bay of late have focused attention on navigation safety in confined waterways. Whenever an oil tanker has a mishap and pollutes coastal waters, the consequences are far-reaching. Shipowners have been forced to take stock of navigational aids, and some now employ computers to help control the operation of their ships.

Merchant ships can make use of computers to control their engines, aid in navigation, keep track of nearby ships, warn of potential collision situations, and monitor cargo, fuel, and electrical equipment. They also perform ship accounting functions such as payroll accounting, stores inventory, management reports, and cargo manifests.

In the late 1950's and early 1960's the U.S. Navy developed a satellite system called Transit.* The system, which uses four satellites in polar orbits, was initially conceived as a navigational aid for Polaris submarines, to provide a worldwide, accurate, all-weather, passive system. Today, Transit provides satellite navigation to ships throughout the world.

Satellite navigation is completely passive, requiring receiving but not transmitting equipment. The satellite beams a precise timing mark and a navigational message that describes the satellite's position at that mark. The computer on a ship at sea uses this information to determine the vessel's precise position.

Satellite navigation is the most accurate method available for obtaining positional fixes at sea. The satellites do not provide continuous signals, but only one signal per orbit, or approximately every two hours. This information is used to update other continuously operating navigational systems which are subject to cumulative errors in relation to time. It also complements the use of Loran, Omega, Decca, and other electronic navigation aids.

The British liner, *Queen Elizabeth II,* was built with the aid of computers and sails with the help of two others. One of these can select the

---

*Also called the Navy Navigation Satellite System (NAVSAT).

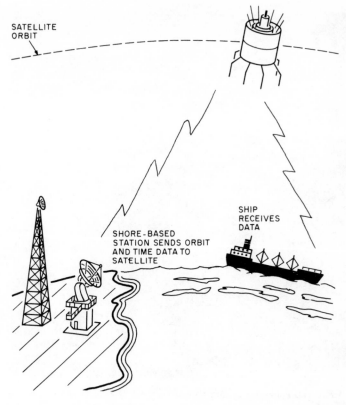

SATELLITE ORBIT

SHORE-BASED STATION SENDS ORBIT AND TIME DATA TO SATELLITE

SHIP RECEIVES DATA

Satellite navigation is used in offshore position fixing, allowing ships to get accurate fix at 120-minute intervals.

proper course for the ship, taking into account the water flow of the various water currents, the weather reports from the earth satellites, and other details. It does not usurp the captain's position, however. When necessary, it provides three choices, and he selects the one he wants. In facing a storm, for instance, the computer will find one route around it, another straight through it, and a third based solely on economic considerations. At the same time, in view of passenger comfort, it will inform the captain just how bad the waves are likely to be and how much discomfort passengers will experience if he chooses the course through the storm. Passenger comfort is also considered in such simple matters as hot water, for instance. The computer monitors the heating of the water and bases the amount of heat required on the time of day and how much hot water is actually being used. As a result, there should still be hot water even if everyone should simultaneously decide to take a hot shower.

A second computer aboard the *Queen* processes navigational information from the Navy Transit satellites.

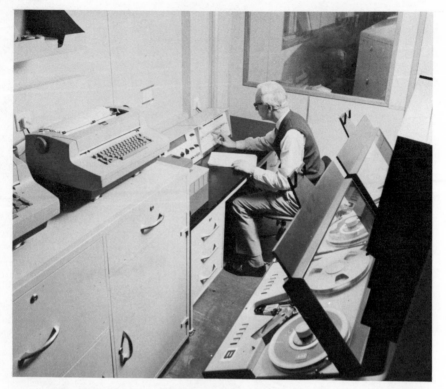

Argus 400 computer system aboard *Queen Elizabeth II*. (*Courtesy,* Cunard Lines)

Simulated Transportation Systems

Computers are used to simulate a variety of transportation systems, especially flight-simulation systems. The latter are used to train and upgrade pilots in the operation of aircraft realistically, safely, and economically without ever leaving the ground. For example, Delta Air Lines' simulator building near Atlanta, Georgia, maintains simulators for the following aircraft: Convair 880's, DC-9's, DC-8's, and L-1011's. Each gives the pilot most of the same sensations that he would encounter in flight. All aircraft controls are simulated, and a system called VAMP (Variable Anamorphic Motion Picture) provides realistic visual effects. Actual landing and take-off scenes are faithfully presented in response to the pilot's manipulation of the controls. The United Air Lines Flight Training Center in Denver, Colorado houses simulators for DC-8's, Boeing 720's, Caravelles, Boeing 737's, Boeing 727's, and Boeing 747's, among others.

Flight simulators make it possible for pilots to become familiar with new aircraft long before they are delivered to the airlines. TWA pilots logged hundreds of computer trips on a Boeing 747 months before the first 747 arrived

Synthetic Flight Training System using a computer-driven display and closed-circuit television portion of an automated flight simulator to permit one instructor to train four helicopter pilots simultaneously. (*Courtesy*, Sanders Associates, Inc.)

on the scene. These simulated trips took the pilots over long-range routes: Los Angeles to Honolulu, Hong Kong to Taipei, and the like. For a simulated Guam to Hong Kong flight, the computer was given such data as the 2,100-mile distance, the Guam runway length of 12,200 feet, the probable winds, and the flight speed. The 4-hour, 13-minute flight was completed in seconds by the computer, which also calculated use of fuel on the climb, cruise, and landing. Computer-printed flight results showed an operating cost per mile of $3.35.

Simulation systems have been used extensively in the Apollo program to simulate actual mission conditions that astronauts would encounter on their flights to and from the moon. To fully satisfy rigid training requirements, the simulator faithfully represents the internal and external environment of space-

Apollo Mission Command Module Simulator and its console area at the Manned Spacecraft Center. (*Courtesy,* NASA)

Computer system at the Manned Spacecraft Center used to supply vital data and predictions during the Apollo 15 moon mission.

craft. According to astronauts who have flown on Apollo missions, the attempted simulation is very close to the actual event. Three simulation engineers at the Simulator Operator Console use a variety of displays, indicators, and controls to operate the simulator, monitor and direct crew activity, provide cues for system management, insert malfunctions and initial conditions, and record flight parameters and reactions of the crew. Though motion is not simulated physically, the actual sensations are provided by the visual system. Realism of the mission is maintained by simulation of aural effects such as those of booster engine and thruster firings, pyrotechnic noises, and by the injection of smoke into the command module to simulate electrical fires resulting from chemical reactions.

Computers are also used to simulate automobile traffic. A system called TRANS (Traffic Network Simulator) evaluates the effect of traffic signal settings on traffic flow in order to optimize their timing. TRANS may also be used to study the effect of other traffic parameters, like one-way streets, left-turn pockets, parking regulations, and left-turn regulations.

Aerospace Transportation System

Although the aerospace transportation system of the National Aeronautics and Space Administration transports only a few people, it is extremely important in that many things learned by flying in space are applicable to more conventional modes of transportation. Hundreds of computers are used in NASA aerospace systems, and many technological advances in the computer field are a direct spinoff from this application.

Recommended Reading

Clark, J.O.E., *Computers At Work,* Grosset & Dunlap, 1971, pp. 24-34, 52-78, 144-151.

Dorf, R.C., *Introduction to Computers and Computer Science,* Boyd & Fraser, 1972, Chap. 17.

Martin, J., and Norman, A.R.D., *The Computerized Society,* Prentice-Hall, 1970, Chap. 11.

Computer Usage: Applications, Weiss, E.A., ed., McGraw-Hill, 1970, Chap. 9.

11

Miscellaneous Jobs for Computers

Earth Resources

The application of computers to the proper management of earth's resources is becoming increasingly important. Today's dilemma can be simply stated: man's potential for consuming is almost endless, and the earth's potential to provide is not. Thus the ultimate goal of earth resources management is to achieve a stable balance between man and his resources. To illustrate how critical this problem is, consider the following: (1) The United States, with 5 percent of the world's population, consumes over 50 percent of the current output of the world's resources, and (2) if everyone now alive consumed petroleum products at the same rate as each U.S. citizen does, the world's known resources would be exhausted in two years.

How can the computer be of help? One way is to manipulate mathematical models formulated by environmentalists. Satellites offer the promise of recording what is happening around the globe, and computers offer the promise of processing the vast amounts of information thus generated so that it can be put to good use. The computer is thus a vital tool for analyzing earth resource projects. For example, if a decision were made to irrigate thousands of square miles of desert to create a new agricultural area, the computer could predict such things as the effects of this undertaking on climate, pollution, population, water resources, and international trade.

The following example illustrates how water pollution is being fought with the aid of the computer. If the city waste treatment plant failed at Dayton, Ohio, how would the dissolved oxygen content of Miami River be affected three miles to the south? Would the pH level of the water be influenced in Middletown if a new manufacturing plant was built six miles upstream in Franklin? Finding answers to questions like these is one of the jobs of the engineers of the Miami Conservancy District in Dayton, Ohio, which is making one of the most detailed and exhaustive studies ever attempted on a river. By determining the factors that

Computer-controlled potato picker that uses X-ray techniques to reject all foreign matter from the crop. (*Courtesy*, Digital Equipment Corp.)

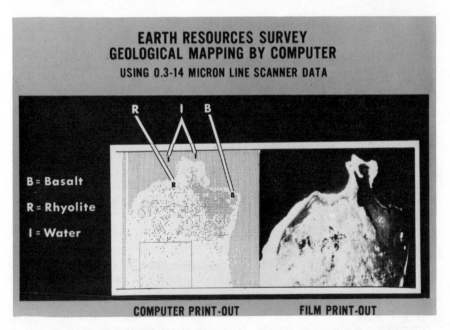

Computer-produced geological map of Pacha Island in Mono Lake, Calif., along with film print-out of region. (*Courtesy*, NASA)

Information about Miami River water is stored on interchangeable disk packs.
(*Courtesy,* National Cash Register Co.)

influence water quality on this heavily used river, officials hope to develop practical means for improving and maintaining high quality levels.

Massive amounts of information being collected from the river will be computer programmed to create a mathematical model of the river. The data will make it possible to simulate the effect of varying conditions, either real or projected.

Quality conditions of the Miami River depend on a complex interaction of the discharge of treated municipal, industrial waste, and agricultural waters and the physical characteristics of the river itself. Because of the great concentration of cities and industries for 130 miles along the banks of the river from Sidney on the north to the Ohio River on the south, it is difficult to develop a realistic program for water quality protection unless the combined effects of the waste loads can be studied.

Water quality study is very different from other hydrology projects. Water conditions, highly affected by light and temperature as well as discharges from factories, community treatment plants, and similar sources, change from minute to minute and from one part of the river to another. An effective mathematical model requires that literally millions of numerical representations be available for processing—a volume of data, calculation, and manipulation that only a computer is equipped to handle. This mass of information must be stored in process-ready format on a disc file. Two interchangeable disc packs mounted on

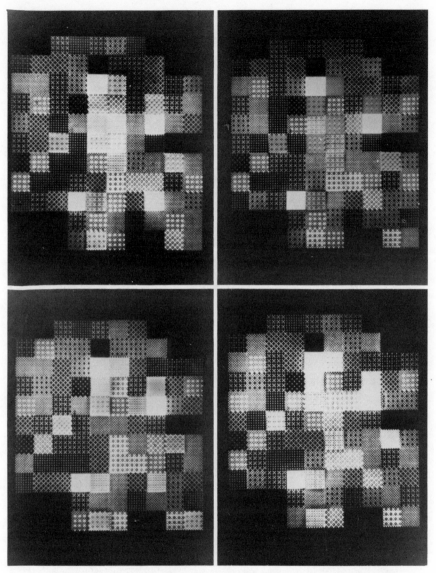

Sequence of computer-generated rainfall-rate patterns at 10-second intervals. Small "patches" corresponding to geographic positions of 93 rain gauges can have any one of 48 computer representations of rain rate: dark for no rain and gradually brightening for increasing rainfall. Each of the four frames maps a rain-storm in the area, and the sequence is like a motion picture. (*Courtesy,* Bell Telephone Laboratories)

this file contain up to 8.4 million characters of data. These packs provide enough capacity to house large segments of a mathematical model within the computer

Data from Tiros-M weather satellite is received, processed, recorded, and disseminated by computers. (*Courtesy,* Varian Associates)

system at any one time and can be changed as the work requires so as to be applicable to the whole length of the waterway.

Monitoring of water quality in the Miami basin calls for a continuing flow of information into and out of the computer. For example, each of the 60 users of the river submits a monthly report that is keypunched and stored. The punched cards indicate the quality of the influent to the plant and the effluent into the river as well as the amount of stream loading. Combined reports give the total volume of loading for any given stretch of stream.

Routine samplings are also taken from various locations along the stream, measuring such conditions as stream flow, air and water temperature, weather conditions, and pH and dissolved oxygen content. Laboratory reports from these samplings will also indicate chemical content—the amount of nitrates, sulfates, phosphates, iron, lead, copper, zinc, and so forth.

One of the big problems is to know just what pollution really does to the river. The computer can help provide the answers. The nature of the stream itself is very important, for a condition that affects the Miami River adversely may have very little influence on some other river and vice versa. For this reason, the work of the ecologists is also very important; data provided by the computer helps them evaluate work that has already been done and project future developments.

Weather Prediction

Using computers for weather prediction, engineers and scientists are now able to anticipate floods, determine where and how to build dams, steer ships safely across oceans, identify hail-laden storms, and reduce shoreline erosion.

In the early days, weather forecasting usually involved solving simple and crude equations plus—plenty of guesswork. Today, computers and weather satellites have greatly improved the accuracy of forecasting. Much of the guesswork has been eliminated by improved mathematical formulas and increased amounts of information.

After Hurricane Beulah devastated the Gulf Coast in 1967, data was collected on the storm, the damage it caused, and its effects on the Rio Grande. By simulating Beulah on the computer with a mathematical model created from this data, weather experts and engineers tried to determine what changes could be made in the Rio Grande flood control system to provide greater protection. The simulation allowed them to test the adequacy of proposed changes.

Among the U.S. satellites used to gather weather data are *Tiros* and *Nimbus*. These satellites revolve around the earth always pointing their television cameras toward its center. The information they transmit is received by ground stations to be processed by computers and then communicated to meteorological agencies.

Computer Dating

What started as a whimsical idea for arranging a Harvard University Dance in 1964 has become the space age alternative of the blind date and the marriage broker. Computer dating involves the process of matching the common known interests between two individuals. An individual (male or female) fills out a questionnaire containing questions such as the following:

BUSINESS AUTOMATION

"Gee! My first computer date! I wonder what he'll be like?"

1. I am: (1) male, (2) female
2. My height is: (1) 5' or shorter, (2) 5'8" or shorter, (3) 5'8" or taller
3. My sense of humor is: (1) excellent, (2) very good, (3) good, (4) just average
4. I am: (1) going to college, (2) not going to college
5. I like to dance: (1) slow, (2) fast, (3) both, (4) neither
6. I enjoy: (1) watching sports, (2) playing sports, (3) both, (4) neither
7. My hair is: (1) short, (2) average, (3) long, (4) very long
8. I am: (1) very athletic, (2) moderately athletic, (3) not athletic
9. I am: (1) very talkative, (2) talkative, (3) average, (4) quiet
10. I prefer dates who are: (1) very talkative, (2) talkative, (3) average, (4) quiet, (5) not important

The list of such questions might be a hundred or more, depending upon the questionnaire used. The information is fed to a computer which compares it with stored information on individuals of the opposite sex. The computer then produces a list of individuals whose descriptions most nearly match each other.

Computer dating was very popular on the college campus during the mid 1960's. Today, several businesses offer such services at large to interested

Computer dating questionnaire.

individuals. How scientific is computer dating? Not very. Despite the lengthy questions designed to probe one's personality, the fact is that the computer can find a person a date all right, but a date is not necessarily a mate. As psychologist Dr. Joyce Brothers put it, "People don't always say what they want. Fred may say he wants a blond who likes to dance but really he would be happiest with a brunette who makes bread." Scientific or not, one business called Operation Match says there have been 125,000 marriages between their customers. There have been, however, five million customers.

Gambling and the Computer

The gambling casino has begun to use computers. A system called Centronics Casino System controls all of its cash, chips, and credit transactions. The system requires that individual transactions involving the sale of chips, the cashing in of chips, the transfer of chips, the issuance of credit, the payment of credit, and the receipt of checks be entered into the computer either through a table keyboard at each gaming table, a cashier's keyboard, or an accounting keyboard. A croupier inserts his identification card and punches in the details of each transaction. The computer controls them all, placing the data into its

Computer Keno system with ticket-writer terminal in the foreground. (*Courtesy*, Ricca Data Systems)

memory and generating the necessary paperwork, vouchers, or transaction listings. No cash, markers, or chips can change hands until the computer generates the paperwork, which takes less than two seconds. A tape shows the nature and amount of each transaction, the table number, and the dealer's identity. The cashier is kept informed of players whose signatures are required and whether to send cash or a credit slip to the table involved. At the end of a shift, and at the end of the day, the casino management gets a statistical summary of profits and losses. At any time during the play, the computer can report the current win or loss of the casino in dollars.

Keno operations have been speeded up by the use of a computer. Keno is a game of Chinese origin in which a player selects up to fifteen numbers out of eighty possible and places a wager. The house draws, at random, twenty numbered balls of ping-pong size from a rotating "fishbowl." A player may win as much as $25,000 on a single wager. A system, called Kenotronic Accounting System, automatically reads player-marked Keno tickets and stores the data in computer storage. When all tickets have been processed, and the random numbers have been selected, the computer instantly prints out the winning ticket numbers with the amount of their winnings, the total amount paid out, and the gross receipts of the game. The system eliminates the inherent problems of hand-written tickets, decreases waiting time between games, and facilitates remote play.

The largest and fastest collector of cash in the nation except for the Internal Revenue Service—the parimutuel betting system—uses computers to minimize betting time, provide greater flexibility for betting operations, and help reduce the burden on racetrack staffs. The parimutuel system compiles betting totals, calculates odds, and performs other bookkeeping operations. It also runs public displays on the track infield and elsewhere. New York City now offers off-track betting via a terminals system as well.

Game Playing with Computers

A number of machines have been specifically built over the years to play games. In the late eighteenth century Baron Wolfgang von Kempelen astounded Europe with an automatic chess-playing machine. It was later found that this machine contained a chess-playing midget. In the nineteenth century Charles Babbage wanted to build a tic-tac-toe machine to help finance the development of his Analytical Engine. In 1914, a Spanish inventor named L. Torres y

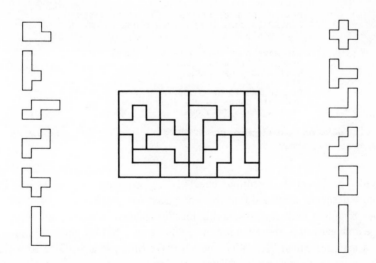

In the game of pentominoes, a player arranges twelve different figures consisting of five contiguous equal squares in a 6 by 10-inch rectangular box. A computer was used to determine that there are more than two thousand different ways of arranging the twelve figures, but the reader will probably be lucky to come up with only one solution different from the one shown.

```
YOU HAVE Q OF SPADES, 9 OF HEARTS.
DEALER SHOWS Q OF CLUBS
HIT?  NO
DEALER HAS 8 OF DIAMONDS, Q OF CLUBS
DEALER'S SCORE IS 18. YOUR SCORE IS 19.
YOU WIN THIS ONE.                    $1.00

YOU HAVE 9 OF DIAMONDS, 9 OF SPADES.
DEALER SHOWS 3 OF DIAMONDS
HIT?  NO
DEALER HAS 4 OF HEARTS, 3 OF DIAMONDS
4 OF CLUBS
2 OF DIAMONDS
5 OF HEARTS
DEALER'S SCORE IS 18. YOUR SCORE IS 18.
THIS ONE'S A TIE.

YOU HAVE A OF CLUBS, J OF CLUBS.
DEALER SHOWS 6 OF CLUBS
YOU HAVE A BLACKJACK                 $3.00

YOU HAVE 2 OF SPADES, 5 OF CLUBS.
DEALER SHOWS Q OF SPADES
HIT?  YES 10 OF SPADES
HIT?  NO
DEALER HAS K OF HEARTS, Q OF SPADES
DEALER'S SCORE IS 20. YOUR SCORE IS 17.
DEALER TAKES THIS ONE.               $2.00

YOU HAVE J OF CLUBS, 4 OF DIAMONDS.
DEALER SHOWS 8 OF HEARTS
HIT?  YES 2 OF DIAMONDS
HIT?  YES 7 OF DIAMONDS
SORRY ABOUT THAT.                    $1.00

YOU HAVE A OF HEARTS, 2 OF CLUBS.
DEALER SHOWS 10 OF DIAMONDS
HIT?  YES 7 OF HEARTS
HIT?  NO
DEALER HAS K OF DIAMONDS, 10 OF DIAMONDS
DEALER'S SCORE IS 20. YOUR SCORE IS 20.
THIS ONE'S A TIE.

YOU HAVE 3 OF HEARTS, 4 OF HEARTS.
DEALER SHOWS K OF SPADES
HIT?  YES 7 OF SPADES
HIT?  NO
DEALER HAS 10 OF CLUBS, K OF SPADES
DEALER'S SCORE IS 20. YOUR SCORE IS 14.
DEALER TAKES THIS ONE.               $2.00
```

Computer printout of games played with a blackjack program. As usual, the player loses money.

Quevedo constructed a genuine chess-playing machine. In the 1930's E. V. Condon designed a special-purpose computer for playing the game of Nim. Claude Shannon built a chess-playing machine named "Caissac" and went on to define how general-purpose computers could be used to play chess. Shannon also built a machine called "NIMWIT" which plays Nim and a machine to solve the ancient puzzle known as the "Tower of Hanoi." Today one may find several special-purpose game-playing machines (such as the tic-tac-toe machine at Disneyland and the roulette, craps, wheel-of-fortune, and blackjack machines in casinos), but game-playing general-purpose computers are perhaps more common.

How does a computer play a game? It may be pitted against a human player as would be done in a game of tic-tac-toe or chess. It may also be directed to generate the solution to a specific game or puzzle, such as the magic square. The computer can also be used as a scorekeeper between two players or teams, as in war games and business games. The most popular form of play for the computer is for it to participate in the game as an active player. In this type of play the human player indicates each of his moves to the computer on an input device such as a teletypewriter or light pen display unit. The computer will then compute its move and report its move to the human being. The report is given on a teletypewriter, line printer, display, or some other output device. The computer also keeps score by recording both its own moves and the human being's moves.

In games where no fixed solution exists, the computer looks several moves ahead, examining all possible combinations of its own moves and those of the opponent, and selecting the move which is most advantageous to it according to some computable criterion for selecting a position. This procedure is followed in chess, checkers, and the Japanese game of GO and somewhat simulates the action of a human player. Naturally there are many different possible moves in games of chess, checkers, and GO, and millions of possible situations result from just a few moves: approximately 10^{120} in chess, 10^{40} in checkers, and 10^{172} in GO. Because of the size of these numbers, a computer cannot analyze in any reasonable amount of time all possible sequences of moves in these games.

The Shape of Things To Come

The garment industry uses computers to grade clothing patterns from a single original model to a full range of dress or suit sizes. After a designer's pattern has been earmarked for production, the next step is to grade it into the different sizes of the buying public. Traditionally, this has been done by hand, generating heavy paper patterns which the fabric cutter uses as templates for cutting larger and smaller sizes.

Pattern grading by computer involves tracing the original pattern with a curve tracer. This device stores the original pattern in computer storage as sets of X-Y coordinates. The computer then uses these coordinates to expand and contract the pattern throughout a complete range of sizes while maintaining the style and fit of the original (see illustration on the next page).

Computers and Newspapers

The newspaper industry has always been slow to change its production methods. It is often said, for example, that a printer from the turn of the century could come into the shop of any present-day American newspaper and go to work without being retrained. The statement is an exaggeration, of course, but there is some truth in it.

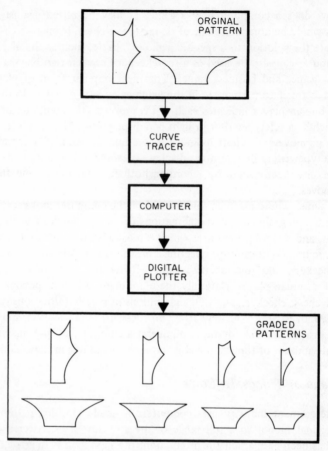

Computerized pattern grading involves tracing the original pattern by a curve tracer. The computer grades this pattern into different sizes and outputs them by means of a digital plotter.

In recent years, however, newspapers have begun to experiment with several new computerized techniques: computer typesetting systems, editing and proof-reading terminals, CRT typesetting machines, and various text composition systems. Publishers everywhere are interested in how computers can help them produce newspapers. Many of them hope to see a time when the entire printing process will be automated. As John H. Perry, Jr., president of Perry Publications, Inc. of West Palm Beach, Florida, put it: "I can visualize a composing room of the future that will automatically compose a page in the newspaper starting from a typewritten page to a finished page without any human hands touching it until it is finished and ready for the press." Such a composing method is still some years away. To bring it about, more reliable optical scanning devices and faster devices for printing are needed.

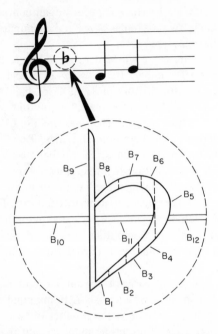

Type and images can be formed on screen of a computer-controlled display. Shown here is musical flat sign composed of many segments called *patches*. (*Courtesy*, Bell Telephone Laboratories)

The Associated Press bureau in Atlanta, Georgia uses a computer-based message preparation and storage system to get news stories to subscribers in seven southeastern states. AP correspondents transmit their news stories to Atlanta by facsimile, which transmits a picture of the reporter's typewritten story. An editor in Atlanta will edit the story if necessary and have the story punched on paper tape. The tape goes directly into a computer, where each line is justified and then stored. As the news day progresses, stories queue up for transmission on the telegraph lines connecting Atlanta with AP newspapers. When the lines are open, the computer transmits the stories over the lines. Subscribers to this system receive both the text of a story and a paper tape. The paper tape can be fed into typesetting machines that automatically reproduce the story it contains. Systems such as this provide an inexpensive way of transmitting information over common communication lines.

The Computer in Mathematics

It has been maintained by enthusiasts that the computer has caused a revolution in mathematical thought. This statement is undoubtedly far too sweeping for, although in applied mathematics many practical results have been achieved, in pure mathematics the computer's main contribution has been of a purely numerical kind. Two examples of using the computer to solve mathematical problems will be considered here.

Perfect numbers are those whose divisors add up to the number itself. For example, 6 is a perfect number. Its divisors—1, 2, and 3—total 6. The next perfect number is 28—with divisors of 1, 2, 4, 7, and 14. Some 20 of these perfect numbers have been known for years, but anything beyond that was once thought to be virtually unattainable. That was true until 1970 when an 18-year-old high school student, Roy Ferguson of Dallas, Texas, used a computer to produce the twenty-first perfect number, a number that contained 5,688 digits. Although its precise determination required large amounts of computer processing time, the FORTRAN program used contained less than 25 statements. Shortly after he found the twenty-first perfect number, Ferguson used a computer at Southern Methodist University to compute the twenty-second and twenty-third perfect numbers. Computing these 5,985- and 7,723-digit numbers required about three hours time on a Digital Equipment Corporation PDP-10 computer.

In 1971, an IBM mathematician, Bryant Tuckerman, used a computer to produce the largest known *prime number*. A prime number is a positive whole number which cannot be written as the product of two smaller factors (other than 1). The numbers 3 and 7 are prime numbers, but 6 and 28, while perfect, are not prime since $6 = 2 \cdot 3$ and $28 = 7 \cdot 4$. The first-occurring prime numbers are 1,2,3,5,7,11,13,17,19,23,29,31,37,41,43,. . . .

This largest known prime number in exponential form is $2^{19,937} - 1$. It took nearly 40 minutes on an IBM System/360 Model 91 computer to produce it. Written out in full the new prime is 6,002 digits long. One can also derive from it a new perfect number, $(2^{19,937} - 1)(2^{19,936})$, which, written out in full, would contain 12,003 digits. Without computer aid it would be unthinkable to produce such large numbers.

Computerized Sports

The application of computers to athletics and sports is developing quite rapidly.* Almost every sport has by now become involved. A computer system costing around $6 million, for example, was used in the 1972 Olympic Games in Munich, Germany. This system played a part in virtually every stage of recording and distributing results. Timing of track events was carried out by a television recorder that recorded a frame for every one-thousandth of a second. The recorder operated under the control of a pair of computers. Some results were fed into the computer manually to be checked for plausibility. Exceptional results, such as new world records, were queried for confirmation.

---

*An excellent article about computerized sports was published in *Datamation,* June 1, 1971, "Sports and EDP . . . It's a New Ballgame," by J. Gerry Purdy.

Olympic swimming trials at Chicago's Portage Park Pool received assist from poolside computer. (*Courtesy,* Burroughs Corp.)

In field events, distances were measured by an optical/electronic device and results immediately transmitted to the computer, which relayed them onto the electronic scoreboards on the field. Athletes and spectators were thus able to see how each competitor stood at any stage in an event, and what changes in the order resulted from each play.

The other major task of the Olympic computers was the control of accommodations and tickets. The 1972 Olympics were certainly the most computerized sports event to date, but look out for the 1976 Olympics in Montreal. Would anyone care to predict how computers will be used in these games?

Computers can make sports more interesting by providing more information to everyone involved. They can also improve athletic performance and quality by providing this information in less time than other methods can.

One of the most widespread applications of computers to athletics has been in football play analysis systems. These systems generate statistical summaries and analyses of the plays of a given football game. The output is examined by the coaches to pinpoint the tendencies of a team. Another football

This computer printout of a Pittsburgh Pirate player is a replica of the one shown on the giant scoreboard of that team. (*Courtesy,* Digital Equipment Corp.)

application for computers is as an aid in the scouting of college players for the pro draft each year. Over half of the professional football teams are members of one of three separate scouting organizations that collect information on thousands of potential professional football players. The first organization, called *TROIK,* operates for the 49ers, Rams, and Cowboys. *BLESTO VIII* operates for a combine of teams including the Bears, Lions, Eagles, Steelers, and Vikings. *CEPO* operates for the Colts, Bills, and Dolphins. Agents of these organizations travel around the country visiting schools and filling out scouting reports. The reports are keypunched onto cards for computer storage. The computer then ranks the players both according to position and independently of position.

Track and field is one of the oldest sport categories in existence, with competitions dating back to the early Olympics in Athens (776 B.C.). Track, unlike football, is not vitally affected by economic concerns since there is virtually no professional track in existence. Although computers had been used to evaluate the scoring system used in track, most applications of the computer to track were first introduced in the 1972 Olympics.

Computer simulation has been used to stage baseball and boxing events. An all-time World Series was held in 1970 in which eight teams competed:

1927 New York Yankees	1955 Brooklyn Dodgers
1929 Philadelphia Athletics	1961 New York Yankees
1942 St. Louis Cardinals	1963 Los Angeles Dodgers
1951 New York Giants	1969 New York Mets

The finals pitted the 1927 New York Yankees against the 1961 Yankees. The winner of that game was the 1927 Yankees. Also in 1970, a computer simulation of a Rocky Marciano–Muhammad Ali fight took place. Who won? Marciano (of course, Ali disagreed).

A very interesting application of computers to sports has taken place in auto racing. The Ontario Motor Speedway (a $4 million installation completed in 1971) uses a giant computer-controlled display board to show the numbers of winning cars. Radio transmitters are installed in each race car and antennas are placed in the roadbed of the track. Every time the car passes over the antenna, a signal is sent to a computer that stores its time (correct to 1/1000 of a second) and other information. Race statistics are made available on the big board display, on CRT display monitors, and as a paper printout.

In Oakland, a computer is used to compile minute statistics during the course of a game and display them on a scoreboard. Each batter's average, for example, is shown when he comes up to bat and reflects his season to data average as of the last time at bat. The scoreboard for the Dallas Cowboys incorporates video data terminals. The computer is programmed to maintain current team and player statistics during the play of the game. At any time during the game, messages may be displayed by the scoreboard director at his discretion. The computer scoreboard, in fact, has become common across the nation.

Recommended Reading

Booth, A.D., *Digital Computers in Action,* Pergamon Press (London), 1965.

Clark, J.O.E., *Computers At Work,* Grosset & Dunlap, 1971, pp. 46-51, 79-83.

Gerald, C.F., *Computers and the Art of Computation,* Addison-Wesley, 1972, Chap. 14.

Hattery, L.H., and Bush, G.P., *Automation and Electronics in Publishing,* Spartan, 1965.

Martin, J., and Norman, A.R.D., *The Computerized Society,* Prentice-Hall, 1970.

Rothman, S., and Mosmann, C., *Computers and Society,* Science Research Associates, 1972.

Spencer, D.D., *Game Playing with Computers,* Hayden, 1968.

Computer Usage: Applications, Weiss, E.A., ed., McGraw-Hill, 1970.

12

Computers and the Future

Trends in Computer Hardware

Computer technology throughout the world has improved at an unbelievably fast pace during the past two decades. In the 1960's computers were used in ways not even envisioned in the 1950's. In the next two decades one can expect the computer to be used in many applications not envisioned today. Every few years a rapid change in computer hardware and technology occurs, thus making older systems obsolete. In this way the computer industry is quite similar to the automobile industry, which replaces its older models each year. By 1980, the value of computing equipment in use may be around 75 billion dollars.

The first all-electric computer, ENIAC (Electronic Numerical Integrator and Computer), contained 19,000 vacuum tubes, weighed about 30 tons, and filled an area of over 1500 square feet (the size of an average three-bedroom home). This enormous device, developed in 1946, could perform 5,000 additions per second. Today computers are much smaller, much lighter, and can perform as many as 100,000,000 additions per second (this rate will be achieved by the computer now being installed by the Atomic Energy Commission at the Lawrence Livermore Laboratory in California). The new machines are more reliable than the old, require less power to operate, and produce considerably less heat. All the early computers had to be placed in air-conditioned rooms. Today computers can be placed anywhere: in an office, in one's home, in an airplane, on a ship, in a missile or spacecraft, in a bank or hospital.

The IBM System/360 Model 195 is an example of a large computer. This machine can process instructions at a rate of one every 54 billionths of a second. In that time, light, traveling at a rate of 186,281 miles a second, can move only 53 feet. The Model 195 can solve 15 problems simultaneously. Its capacity would allow the literary content of a library with more than 3 million books to be stored, and it would be able to locate and read any one of these books in less than one second. This multi-million dollar computer can be used in a variety of

IBM System/360 Model 195 computer can solve fifteen problems simultaneously. (*Courtesy,* McDonnell Douglas Automation Co.)

applications—weather predictions, airline reservations, space exploration, and so
forth.

Other large computers are the Control Data Corporation 7600, the Illiac 4,
and the Univac 1110. The CDC 7600 is a large "number cruncher" that is used
for scientific work. The Illiac 4 is essentially 64 computers operating in parallel.
It is being assembled at the Ames Research Center in California by Burroughs
Corporation. This 25-million-dollar machine, which was designed to solve complex scientific problems, will one day be able to handle more than 200,000,000
instructions per second. When fully operational, it may prove to be the world's
fastest computer. The Univac 1110, one in a series of machines by the developer
of Univac I (the world's first commercial computer) is designed to process a wide
variety of application: business, scientific, educational, and so forth.

In contrast with the large computers are the *minicomputers*. These machines cost only a few thousand dollars, are about the size of a suitcase, and
can perform operations similar to the large computers at rates approximating as
many as 600,000 additions per second. What is the future of minicomputers?
Frost and Sullivan, a computer industry research firm, claims that the value of
yearly minicomputer shipments will grow by more than 200 percent between
the end of 1971 and 1978, thus growing to $820 million. It also predicted that

PDP-11 minicomputers being readied for shipment. (*Courtesy,* Digital Equipment Corp.)

there would be 150,000 minicomputers in operation at the end of 1978. These small machines should find widespread use in high schools, hospitals, and small businesses.

Most computers today use magnetic-core memories to store data. Within the next few years integrated-circuit memories are expected to be common. It is believed that these memories, called LSI (Large Scale Integration) memories, will bring about a tenfold cost-performance factor by the mid 1970's. The primary characteristic of tomorrow's computers will thus be much the same as today's: an improved price/performance ratio.

Future computers will probably make extensive use of *firmware;* that is, special programs (called microprograms) within the hardware that will be able to simulate many types of machines. When this revolution occurs, it will make programming a computer and conversion from one computer to another much easier. Users will simply utilize a basic language instruction that will be interpreted through hardware (using a firmware concept) to emulate other machines.

Various companies are now experimenting with *laser computers.* One firm has announced that it is developing a laser computer capable of 50 trillion

Integrated circuits are diffused into surface of silicon chip measuring less than an eighth of an inch square. Each chip contains 664 individual components (diodes, transistors, etc.) and provides 64 memory storage cells. (*Courtesy,* IBM Corp.)

(50,000,000,000,000) bits of storage and of accessing stored data in 20 nanoseconds (billionths of a second). In 1970, the Japan Telegraph and Telephone Company announced the development of a memory that utilizes a laser for printing information on film and in the subsequent read-out. This "hologram memory" is capable of accommodating the entire Tokyo metropolitan telephone directory (3,800 pages) on 16 pieces of film, each measuring 5 inches square. One can definitely expect more usage of the laser in the memory hierarchy of future computer systems.

It seems reasonable to predict that future computers will be faster, more reliable, cheaper, and easier to use. In order to simplify them, one can expect computer manufacturers to develop new man/machine interface devices. Widespread employment of voice-recognition units and optical readers can be expected in the late 1970's. Devices such as the PICTUREPHONE (developed by Bell Telephone laboratories) and mini-terminals will help simplify data communications with computers.

A tap on the controls of a PICTUREPHONE set may one day allow a businessman to have displayed before him vital information serviced by computer. (*Courtesy,* Bell Telephone Laboratories)

The future user of the PICTUREPHONE set can use it as a desk calculator, keying numbers into the remote computer to which it is linked with his TOUCH-TONE telephone buttons; the computer will then perform the calculation and display the answer on his videotelephone screen. In addition to human/computer communications, the PICTUREPHONE will also be used for normal face-to-face conversation.

Credit card readers, keyboard numbering devices, and small display terminals will undoubtedly be widely employed in future computers. A simple mini-terminal consists of a display used in conjunction with a touch-tone telephone. This display might be limited to displaying 20 to 100 characters or even just ten- or twelve-digit numbers. Simple terminals such as this could be used in low-cost computer communication systems, the type that might be found in the 1980-1990 household.

Cathode-ray-tube displays will be much more common in future computer applications, and the cost of these devices should decrease considerably. The Plasma Tube, another type of display device, can be expected to be introduced as a low-cost terminal for computer systems during the late 1970's.

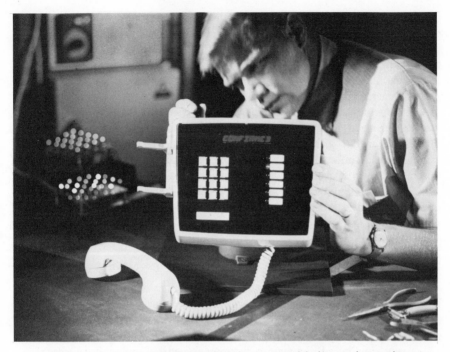

Shown here is a luminescent semiconductor material that works on tiny currents, requiring no power except what comes over the telephone line. One possible use is suggested by the appearance of the word "confirmed" on the telephone instrument—as it might, for instance, if a computer were to signal back confirmation of a bank deposit after a touch-tone push-button request. (*Courtesy,* Bell Telephone Laboratories)

When Christopher Columbus set foot in the New World in 1492, he did not know where he was nor how he got there. It took the world years to learn of his courageous journey. When Neil Armstrong stepped upon the surface of the moon in 1969, he knew exactly where he was, having followed a precisely preplanned route, and the entire world was watching him. In less than five hundred years man's ability to communicate has advanced from its most primitive forms to an astounding level of sophistication.

Computer centers are now being connected to one another via communication facilities. An airline reservations office in Paris, France, can communicate with a computer center in New York via satellite. Large companies can link facilities on opposite sides of the Pacific Ocean.

This developing relationship between computer and telecommunications technology is one of the most important events of our times. The two technologies complement each other; in combination their power is multiplicative, not additive. Computers will one day control immense communication switching centers and these in turn will make available the power of computers to millions of users in remote locations. The present trend toward large-scale, time-shared computers and the development of advanced, so-called "intelligent" terminals seem to indicate that, within the next decade, a large portion of the computers used will be communications-oriented.

The major computer problems of the future will be carryovers from present times. First, there is the people problem: the need to teach students the use of computer processing techniques and to train vast numbers, from minorities in particular, to become productive members of the computer industry. Then there are the social implications of private and governmental data banks, vast nationwide information networks, and the threats they pose, if any, to the privacy of individuals. And with data traffic exceeding voice traffic in the 1970's, data communications faces the problem of overloaded and unreliable transmission lines, and this could seriously hamper the growth of computer processing.

Future Software Systems

It is doubtful if many major software functions will be developed in the next few years. Complex operating systems for machines such as the IBM System/360, Control Data 7600, and Univac 1110 have been designed to meet user's needs for quite a time to come. In other words the software designers have adequately specified all the major functions needed for applications foreseeable in the immediate future.

Programming languages are the primary means by which a person communicates with a computer. The use of current programming languages is not likely to change drastically for a number of years. In 1980, users will probably still be using FORTRAN, COBOL, BASIC, AND PL/I. One may expect to see less usage of ALGOL 60 in the next decade, however, although this language does not have widespread usage even today. (ALGOL has considerably more usage in Russia and European countries than in the United States.)

As computers become more commonplace in schools, homes, and businesses, one can expect more people to learn computer languages. Within the next decade, BASIC or some such language will very likely have widespread usage in high schools. For the distant future, we should expect to see the development and use of natural languages (for example, English) as well as languages designed for specific application areas (for example, languages for solving medical problems, for solving educational problems, for solving engineering problems, and the like).

Recently, a number of researchers have designed and implemented "two-dimensional" programming languages (picture- and symbol-oriented) as opposed to the above-mentioned "one-dimensional" languages (text- and character-oriented). These may become of increasing importance in man-machine communication.

In future computers, one can also expect that many functions now performed by software will be implemented by *microprograms* in a read-only computer memory (firmware).

Future Uses of Computers

Science fiction is rapidly evolving into fact. The computer has your number and may even be watching you. It is safe to assume that there is no aspect of human life that is not in some way affected by behind-the-scenes computers. A computerized society is no longer just a possibility; it is almost here today.

Automation will continue to grow as a way of life because man will always devote much of his efforts to finding new ways to accomplish or circumvent monotonous and laborious tasks, especially those not requiring his full ability as a human being. Have you ever wondered what life will be like in the year 2001? This author believes that automation will play an almost unbelievable part in everyone's life.

Do you believe that unmanned ships will sail across the Atlantic and Pacific Oceans in the year 2001? Science fiction or logical possibility? Considering the inherent risks involved in making predictions, it might be safe to say science fiction. However, because it is stimulating to speculate about the unknown, and also because there is some security in this age of rapidly changing technology, this author calls it a logical prediction (assuming that no nuclear war occurs beforehand).

Let us now examine what life may be like in the year 2001. Many of these predictions will undoubtedly prove to be in error, but perhaps they will show us how the evolving use of computers may affect our lives.

Transportation

It was just 24 hours and a few minutes since he left the shores of Italy; now the ship's captain saw the skyline of New York City before him. Soon control of his giant merchant ship would be assumed by harbor control. Automatically the ship would be guided, at high speeds, through the ship channel to the docking and unloading center. Here the ship would be completely unloaded by means of a computer-controlled unloading system directly onto transportation devices for immediate shipment to various points throughout the United States. The unloading operation would take two hours. Within an additional two hours the ship would be on its way back to Europe, or some other destination, fully loaded with cargo, streaking across the ocean at better than 100 knots without a crew busy at its controls. This was the last of the manned trips. The computer would be in complete control of the ship on all future voyages. Using inputs from radars, satellites, sonars, and other naviga-

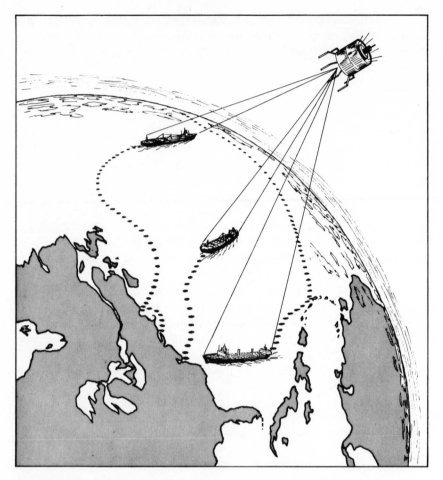

A ship's propulsion and maneuvering will one day be computer-monitored
from space and altered whenever necessary to provide the safest and calmest
route.

tional equipment, the computer would control ship operations as an electronic
captain. The year is 2001—the age of automated transportation systems.

Ships now communicate with shore stations and other ships using satellites
in synchronous orbits (approximately 20,000 nautical miles above the earth).
Each of these satellites is in view of one-third of the earth's surface. Shipowners
now monitor the operations of their complete fleet. Their computer-controlled
display consoles reveal at a glance the locations and status of all ships. The ship's
position (latitude and longitude), speed, course, remaining fuel, engine status,
electrical system status, cargo status, and weather conditions are all communicated to the computer system every few minutes. It performs a few calcula-

```
SHIP 1    STATUS NO. 4 – GENERAL INFORMATION

OWNER – GRANT SHIPPING COMPANY
COUNTRY – USA
SHIP'S POSITION
    LATITUDE:  30:18
    LONGITUDE:  47:20
SHIP'S COURSE – 082°
SHIP'S SPEED – 14.3 KNOTS
SHIP'S DESTINATION – CHERBOURG
FUEL REMAINING – 8,000 BBLS
ENGINE ROOM STATUS – 91 RPM, STEAM PRES 540, NO FAILURES
ELECTRICAL SYSTEM STATUS
    SENSOR 126 FAILED
AUTOMATED SUBSYSTEMS
    RADAR NO. 2 IN USE
    FATHOMETER NO. 1 IN USE
WEATHER
    WIND – 260°  21 KN       SEA STATE – 3
    SWELL – WLY MOD          SKY – CLOUDY
    TEMP – 96°               HUM – 47%
```

Ship status report as it would be presented on a computer-controlled display device.

tions and updates the ship's position on the display console. Gone are the days when a ship is "lost at sea."

Surface transportation systems are now available that permit speeds of 250 mph through densely populated cities. Computers are used to design, test, and run these systems. Their bullet-shaped vehicles produce almost no pollutant by-products and are relatively vibration-free. Some of them are equipped with LIM (Linear Induction Motor) motors, which have no wearing parts like gears or bearings. The LIM is operated on alternating current created by electromagnetic fields.

Computers now handle most of the operating details of jetliners, allowing the captain of the ship to keep watch only for unusual occurrences. Computers switch equipment on and off, control aircraft centers of gravity, communicate with other airplane computers enroute, determine the plane's proper speed and altitude, run through preflight checklists, perform automatic takeoffs and landings. The onboard computer takes account of winds, storms, temperature, and other aircraft. When landing, the computer automatically adjusts the speed and angle of descent of the plane so that a perfect landing can be made without any action on the part of the pilot. Maintenance computers give advance notice of needed repairs or replacement of aircraft components and have practically eliminated flight delays or cancellation of flights because of mechanical problems.

Computers have made flying in the year 2001 very safe. They have minimized the possibility of mid-air collisions. They keep track of planes in the same air corridor and calculate the distance between, and direction of, all of them. If the speed and direction of any two planes indicate that a collision is likely, the computer alerts the pilots to the fact that instructions are being prepared to avoid the danger. Within seconds, the computer will advise the pilots of the corrective maneuvers to take.

As the passenger stands in front of the automatic ticket vendor, he is quickly guided through the necessary steps to purchase a ticket by a series of computer-controlled lighted instructions that are sequentially illuminated. During the few seconds it takes for the machine to encode, print, and bond the ticket, the instruction, "Please wait for ticket," is displayed.

Medicine

In 2001 all large hospitals are using centralized computer systems to perform a considerable amount of patient care. A patient entering the hospital is admitted, diagnosed, and monitored by the computer. Electroencephalogram (brain-wave recording) analysis is performed by computer. Electrocardiograms (heart waveforms) are read and interpreted accurately by computer. Phonocardiograms (heart sounds and murmurs) are processed and analyzed by computer. The timing and relative amplitudes of heart sounds are displayed on a CRT display along with the onset, duration, relative amplitudes, and relative frequency information of any systolic or diastolic murmurs which have been detected.

Most doctors have display terminals connected to medical information banks for consultation purposes.

Computers are now performing surgery—a kidney transplant, say—without intervention by a human surgeon. In an article by Dr. Robert Fondiller, a computer-controlled robot, whom he named Dr. Sawbones, operates at lightning speed, a speed almost too fast for the human eye to follow.*

Robots

In the year 2001, robots other than Dr. Sawbones will be walking, making decisions, and thinking, as it were, for themselves. Their minds are composed of programmed computers. They use television-like cameras for eyes to send inputs

---

*"In the Year 2001: Surgery by Computer," *Computers and Automation,* June 1970, pp. 36-40.

to the computer. For example, if a robot on an exploration trip bumps into an obstacle which it has not previously sensed, the television camera and cat-whisker antennas (wire sensors) send data to the computer that in effect ask, "What do I do now?" The computer then switches to an "I'll-walk-around-it" or "Let-me-take-a-look" program.

Robots are used primarily to perform tasks that are boring, dangerous, or have to be performed in hostile environments, such as the floor of the ocean. When NASA sends a space vehicle to Mars, robots will be the first to explore this dangerous terrain.

Computers in the Home

A typical new home in the year 2001 is similar to that of Mr. and Mrs. Universe. This home contains three bedrooms, a family room, kitchen, two bathrooms, and a large play room. Located in the kitchen is a family control center, the heart of which is a computer. There is a keyboard input device, a voice recognition device, and a display device. Mrs. Universe (or Mr. Universe, if he's the family cook) uses the center to conjure up nutritionally balanced, tasty,

Small computer used as a home control center. (*Courtesy,* Digital Equipment Corp.)

```
1st DAY OF YOUR COMPUTERIZED MENU PLAN          2nd DAY OF YOUR COMPUTERIZED MENU PLAN

BREAKFAST           LUNCH                       BREAKFAST           LUNCH

TOMATO JUICE        HOMEMADE POTATO SOUP        GRAPEFRUIT JUICE    PEANUT BUTTER AND JELLY
SCRAMBLED EGGS      SALTED CRACKERS             WHEAT CEREAL WITH MILK  SANDWICHES
CINNAMON TOAST      CELERY AND CARROT STICKS    MILK, COFFEE        APPLE
HOT COCOA           MILK, TEA                                       COOKY
                                                                    MILK, TEA
DINNER              TIP:                        DINNER              TIP:

PORK STEAK WITH ROSEMARY  SHOULDER PORK STEAK COSTS   GLAZED CHICKEN WINGS  BUY WHOLE CHICKENS WHEN
BROILED APPLE RINGS LESS THAN LOIN OR CENTER   CRANBERRY SAUCE     ON SALE AND LEARN TO CUT
RICE                CUT CHOPS; COOK JUST AS     BREAD               THEM UP YOURSELF; YOU'LL
GREEN BEANS         TENDER WHEN SIMMERED OR     CARROTS             SAVE PENNIES A POUND.
TAPIOCA PUDDING     BAKED.                      ORANGE GELATIN
MILK, TEA, COFFEE                               MILK, COFFEE, TEA


3rd DAY OF YOUR COMPUTERIZED MENU PLAN          4th DAY OF YOUR COMPUTERIZED MENU PLAN

BREAKFAST           LUNCH                       BREAKFAST           LUNCH

FORTIFIED ORANGE    BEAN SOUP                   GRAPEFRUIT HALVES   GRILLED CHEESE SANDWICHES
  BEVERAGE          CRACKERS                    FRIED EGGS          APPLE AND PEAR
OATMEAL WITH MILK   CARROT STICKS               TOASTED ENGLISH MUFFINS  MILK, TEA
MILK, COFFEE        MILK, TEA                     WITH MARGARINE
                                                MILK, COFFEE
DINNER              TIP:                        DINNER              TIP:

BEEF STEW           SUBSTITUTE LAMB OR VEAL     MANWICH SKILLET MEAL  USE LOW COST GROUND BEEF
PEACH AND COTTAGE CHEESE  IN THE STEW IF THEY ARE   TOSSED GREEN SALAD  TO MAKE SOUPS AND CHILI;
COOKIES             ON SPECIAL.                 WARMED CORN TORTILLAS  AFTER BROWNING ALWAYS
MILK, COFFEE, TEA                               BAKED CUSTARD       DRAIN EXCESS FAT.
                                                MILK, COFFEE, TEA
```

Computer printout of four meal plans.

eye-pleasing meal plans. She simply supplies the computer with an appropriate code for any of several major food categories. The computer then causes a printout with a full dinner menu planned around entrées such as ham, beef, chicken, trout, lobster, veal, lamb, pork, game, eggs, cheese, and the like. For finicky or allergy-prone diners, substitutions can be obtained by entering additional codes. Mrs. Universe is always free to place new menus in the computer's memory.

Mrs. Universe can also use the center for typing her shopping lists, writing letters, calculating requirements for drapery material, and obtaining suggestions for rearranging room furniture.

Mr. Universe uses the computer to keep track of his investments, to prepare tax reports, to take care of his checkbook accounting, and to solve problems related to his work. For example, he can use the computer to prepare budgets and manpower forecasts for his different business projects. He, like the rest of the family, may also use the computer in his spare time to learn, say, German. The computer retrieves from its memory a teaching program for German, remembering where he left off at the end of the last lesson. The German lessons are programmed to proceed at just the pace that matches his learning rate.

The computer center can drive clocks throughout the house, control the air conditioning and heating system, change television channels at predetermined times, control the stereo music center, open and close doors and windows, and perform family medical diagnoses.

The Universe children, Mars and Space, can also use the computer center. Mars is in elementary school and can check all his arithmetic and language problems by computer. Space, who is in college, can use the computer as a homework aid in practically all his courses. When their lessons are done, the boys can play a game of chess or nim with the computer.

Education

In 2001 small classroom computers are commonplace in all schools: elementary, secondary, and college. Students learn to program computers at an early age and use them throughout their educational careers. Since most families own a home computer, students are expected to use theirs to help them with homework. Computer-assisted instruction (CAI), in which the computer presents tutorial and drill practice information to the student, is a feature of all schools. Libraries are computer-automated and offer even small schools vast repositories of information.

Information Systems

Computers linked to common information banks are now commonplace in law and medicine as well as educational institutions. Criminal justice information systems allow all allied organizations to share information, expand local data files, and analyze interdependent problems such as manpower utilization and court docketing. Medical information systems provide doctors and hospitals with a central source of up-to-date data concerning all known diseases and medical procedures. School terminals connected to a central educational system allow access to vast amounts of general information. Book libraries have become obsolete for obtaining such information.

Space

In the year 2001 there will undoubtedly be a sizeable computer-controlled operation on the moon, and it is entirely possible that man will have flown to the outer planets. A manned Mars landing may even occur around the turn of the century.

Miscellaneous

Cities of the year 2001 are designed with the aid of computers. Mathematical models of atmospheric pollution patterns are used to predict where heavy industry and new population centers should be located to minimize environmental damage and optimize healthful living conditions. Small computers, about the size of a watch, have become available to everyone. These computers cost only about fifty dollars (at the dollar's current value).

Conclusion

The preceding chapters have described many applications of computers today and speculated about some of the uses to which they may be put in the future. The field of application of computers is continually increasing, and eventually there will be few kinds of endeavor that will not have some sort of computer aid. The mere existence of computers increases man's capabilities manyfold. By using these powerful machines, he may be able to solve many social and technical problems that now look almost hopeless. At the same time, one should realize that it is man himself who will always be in control. After all, he can always turn the computer switch OFF!

Recommended Reading

Joslin, E.O., *Management and Computer Systems*, College Readings Inc., Arlington, Va., 1970, pp. 323-332.

Dorf, R.C., *Introduction to Computers and Computer Science*, Boyd & Fraser, 1972, Chap. 19.

Expanding Use of Computers in the 70's: Markets, Needs, Technology, Gruenberger, F., ed., Prentice-Hall, 1971.

Martin, J., and Norman, A.R.D., *The Computerized Society*, Prentice-Hall, 1970.

Nikolaieff, G.A., *Computers and Society*, H.W. Wilson, 1970.

Rothman, S., and Mosmann, C., *Computers and Society*, Science Research Associates, 1972, Chap. 15.

Parkhill, D.F., *The Challenge of the Computer Utility*, Addison-Wesley, 1966, Chap. 8.

The Computer Impact, Taviss, I., ed., Prentice-Hall, 1970, pp. 289-297.

A Prose Glossary

Glossaries of technical terms are very often of little use to the novice since their alphabetic order does not reflect any other logical structure. Attempted here is a glossary* arranged in a more or less logical fashion, with an index (pages 187-188) to help the user find a particular term. If the definition does not shed sufficient light, the context may.

1	A COMPUTER is a machine for performing complex processes on
2	information without manual intervention. ANALOG COMPUTERS
3	perform this function by directly measuring continuous physical
4	quantities such as electrical voltages. The best-known analog computer
5	is a slide rule. DIGITAL COMPUTERS represent numerical quantities
6	by discrete electrical states which can be manipulated logically and
7	hence arithmetically. Digital computers are sometimes referred to as
8	ELECTRONIC DATA PROCESSING MACHINES, EDP, or PROC-
9	ESSORS. In order to distinguish the actual physical equipment from
10	the programs which extend its usefulness, the former is called
11	HARDWARE.
12	The CENTRAL PROCESSOR UNIT (CPU) or MAIN FRAME is the
13	portion of the computer which performs the calculations and deci-
14	sions; the MEMORY or STORAGE is the part in which the data and
15	programs are stored. The CORE MEMORY is the main memory of
16	most modern machines; it is normally the only memory directly accessi-
17	ble to the CPU. Its name derives from its composition: small ferrite rings
18	called CORES. The computer may have additional memory devices;
19	information is transferred between these and the core memory. The
20	most usual such memories are MAGNETIC DRUMS (spinning cylinders
21	with a magnetizable recording surface) and MAGNETIC DISCS (flat
22	spinning discs with magnetizable surfaces).
23	The capability of memory devices is measured in capacity and speed
24	of access. The STORAGE CAPACITY of a memory is measured in
25	WORDS (also called CELLS or REGISTERS) which are usually of fixed
26	length, consisting of from 8 to 64 bits. This number is called the
27	machine's WORD LENGTH. A BIT (binary digit) is the minimum unit of
28	information storage and has only two possible values. Capacity can also
29	be measured in BYTES, units of six or eight bits, each representing one
30	alphabetic, numeric, or special symbol.

---

*Adapted from "Computers on Campus," copyright 1967, by the American Council on Education, Washington, D.C., with permission.

31   ACCESS SPEED of a memory is the time it takes for the processor
32   to obtain a word from memory. Core, drum, and disc memories
33   provide RANDOM ACCESS as any word can be obtained at any time
34   without regard to its serial order. Tape memories use SERIAL ACCESS,
35   in which the words pass one at a time as they move past the station
36   where they may be accessed. Speed is usually spoken of in terms of
37   MILLISECONDS (m) (thousandths of a second), MICROSECONDS (μ)
38   (millionths of a second), or NANOSECONDS (n) (billionths of a second).
39   One nanosecond is the time required for light to travel approximately
40   one foot.
41   The central processor and the memory constitute the computer per
42   se; to get data and programs into the machine and the results out are
43   the role of the INPUT/OUTPUT EQUIPMENT or I/O.
44   INPUT DEVICES convert information to a form in which it can be
45   stored in the computer's memory. The commonest form of input is
46   the PUNCHED CARD or HOLLERITH CARD (after its inventor). In-
47   put devices which accept cards are called CARD READERS and the
48   function they perform is commonly called READING, as is that of all
49   input devices. Cards have 80 COLUMNS with 12 possible punch posi-
50   tions; normally, each column is used to represent one character. A set of
51   cards is called a DECK. Another form of input is PUNCHED PAPER
52   TAPE—continuous tape approximately one inch wide, with holes
53   punched across its width to represent characters or numeric quantities.
54   MAGNETIC INK CHARACTER READERS have come to be used for
55   input, particularly in banking; they can interpret characters printed with
56   a special ink. More recently, OPTICAL SCANNERS have appeared,
57   which can read clearly printed or typed material of given type fonts.
58   OUTPUT DEVICES usually include a CARD PUNCH (which converts
59   the characters stored in memory to punched holes in a card), a TAPE
60   PUNCH (which performs the same function for punched paper tape),
61   and a LINE PRINTER (which prints numerals, letters, and other char-
62   acters of conventional design on continuous rolls of paper). Passing
63   information to these devices is referred to as WRITING. Recent addi-
64   tions to the output family include the DISPLAY DEVICE which exhibits
65   readable characters or graphic information on the face of a CATHODE
66   RAY TUBE or CRT. These images must be read at once, of course,
67   since they are not permanent.
68   Information which can be taken away in permanent form (such as
69   by output line printer) is called HARD COPY. A PLOTTER is an
70   output device which, under computer control, can draw continuous lines
71   or curves on paper, thus producing graphs, maps, etc., in hard copy.
72   MAGNETIC TAPE is widely used both as a form of memory and
73   input/output. It can be stored conveniently away from the machine and
74   can be read or written by the computer if it is put on a TAPE DRIVE

75 attached to the computer. It is the fastest type of I/O and the slowest
76 type of memory except when used for serial reading.
77   I/O devices connected directly to the computer memory and under
78 control of the CPU are spoken of as being ON-LINE. They are placed
79 OFF-LINE when they are used to perform independent functions. For
80 example, it is common to convert information between punched cards
81 and magnetic tape off-line. Some devices are always off-line. These are
82 PERIPHERAL EQUIPMENT and are generally called collectively UNIT
83 RECORD EQUIPMENT (formerly known as EAM). They are fre-
84 quently used independently of the computer and in fact antedate
85 computers by many years. The most common are the KEYPUNCH,
86 used to punch cards, the REPRODUCER, which makes copies of decks
87 of cards, and the SORTER, which places cards in different bins as a
88 function of which holes are punched. In some recent systems, another
89 on-line input/output device has been added, the CONSOLE or TER-
90 MINAL. Its purpose is to allow the user to interact directly with the
91 machine, and usually consists of a typewriter-like keyboard, and either
92 a typewriter-like printing mechanism or another display device for
93 output.
94   Information is stored in the computer's memory in the form of the
95 presence or absence of a magnetic field. A collection of such "yes or
96 no" physical states is usually thought of as a BINARY NUMBER (a
97 number whose only possible digits are 0 and 1). Depending on con-
98 text, such numbers can have many meanings; in this sense, the
99 numbers are CODED. They can be interpreted as numeric quantities,
100 CHARACTERS (letters, digits, punctuation marks) or as IN-
101 STRUCTIONS or COMMANDS which will direct the computer to
102 perform its basic functions (add, compare, read, etc.).
103   A set of instructions to perform a specified function or solve a
104 complete problem is called a PROGRAM. The computer performs such
105 instructions sequentially. However, as the computer can modify the
106 data in its memory, it can also modify its program. This capability to
107 modify its own directions is a case of the engineering principle called
108 FEEDBACK, the modification of future performance on the basis of
109 past performance. It is because of this distinctive feature that modern
110 digital computers are sometimes called STORED-PROGRAM COM-
111 PUTERS. Parts of programs are sometimes called ROUTINES or
112 SUBROUTINES. Subroutines which perform generally useful functions
113 are sometimes combined into a subroutine LIBRARY, usually on
114 magnetic tape. Copies of relevant subroutines will be added to a
115 program automatically and hence need not be developed by hand.
116 Single instructions in a program are sometimes called STEPS. When a
117 sequence of program steps is operated repeatedly, the process is called
118 a LOOP. Certain instructions compare two quantities and select either

119   of two program paths on the basis of the result: these are called
120   BRANCHING instructions.
121   The data on which a program acts are usually structured into
122   TABLES. Individual values which control the operation of programs
123   or subroutines are PARAMETERS. An organized collection of infor-
124   mation in the computer or on tape is called a FILE, like the or-
125   ganized set of papers in a file cabinet. A DATA BASE or DATA
126   BANK is a large and complex set of tables which describe some as-
127   pect of the world outside of the computer (a library catalog, a student
128   record file, a budget).
129   A PROGRAMMER is a person who converts a problem into a set
130   of directions to a computer to solve it. The function is sometimes
131   broken down into several parts, particularly if the problem is very
132   complex. The task of stating the problem in a clear and unambigu-
133   ous form is performed by an ANALYST or SYSTEM ANALYST.
134   The technique of specifying methods of solution for mathematical prob-
135   lems is MATHEMATICAL ANALYSIS or NUMERICAL ANALYSIS. A
136   specific procedure for solving a problem is an ALGORITHM. The process
137   of writing the detailed step-by-step instructions for the computer to
138   follow is CODING, done by a CODER.
139   After a program is written, it is tested by letting it perform its
140   function in the computer on test data to which the proper solution is
141   known. This process is CODE-CHECKING or DEBUGGING. The coder
142   will also produce some descriptions of this program and how it
143   operates so that others may understand how it works, in case at a
144   future date, it is necessary to modify it. This DOCUMENTATION may
145   include a FLOW CHART: a graphic description or diagram of the
146   various paths and branches followed by the program.
147   The repertory of instructions available to the programmer for a
148   specific computer is that computer's MACHINE LANGUAGE. Other
149   HIGHER-ORDER LANGUAGES have been developed to help the
150   programmer by simplifying the tedious aspects of writing machine
151   language; these are also called HIGHER-LEVEL LANGUAGES or
152   PROCEDURE-ORIENTED LANGUAGES or POL's. Commonly used
153   POL's are FORTRAN, ALGOL, and COBOL; the first two were
154   devised mainly for scientific computation and the latter for business
155   data processing. A new type is represented by LIST-PROCESSING
156   LANGUAGES; because of greater flexibilities in dealing with data,
157   these languages are particularly useful in nonnumeric computations
158   such as are frequently involved in research. Their particular virtues are
159   most apparent in HEURISTIC PROCESSES: methods where the pre-
160   cise method of solution is not spelled out but is discovered as the
161   program progresses and as it evaluates its progress toward an ac-
162   ceptable solution. Programming languages are generally referred to as

163   ARTIFICIAL LANGUAGES, and human languages such as English are
164   distinguished as NATURAL LANGUAGES.
165   Programs which convert higher-order languages into machine
166   language are called COMPILERS; programs which perform similar
167   functions but at a much simpler level are ASSEMBLERS. The term
168   TRANSLATOR is used sometimes for compilers, but it is used less
169   frequently because of the possible confusion with programs which
170   perform translation between natural or artificial languages. INTER-
171   PRETERS do not compile the entire program but translate and per-
172   form one statement of the program at a time; effectively, they per-
173   form both functions—compiling and running a program.
174   SOFTWARE is the term used to refer to the totality of programs
175   and procedures available on a computer; sometimes it is used more
176   specifically to mean those programs of general usefulness (such as
177   compilers) which are available to all users. These are sometimes called
178   UTILITY PROGRAMS. All machines today have OPERATING
179   SYSTEMS to aid the user (and the operator) in sequencing jobs,
180   accounting, and calling up other utility programs. Operating systems or
181   programs are also called CONTROL PROGRAMS, SUPERVISORS, or
182   EXECUTIVES.
183   APPLICATIONS are the problems to which a computer is applied;
184   the names for most common applications are self-explanatory, but
185   some are not. A SIMULATION is the representation of a real or
186   hypothetical system by a computer process; its function is to indicate
187   system performance under various conditions by program performance.
188   INFORMATION RETRIEVAL is the name applied to processes which
189   recover or locate information in a collection of documents. An
190   INFORMATION MANAGEMENT SYSTEM helps a user maintain a
191   data base, modify it, and get reports from it. It is usually defined as a
192   GENERAL-PURPOSE DEVICE; this means that it can accommodate a
193   large range of applications. A MANAGEMENT INFORMATION
194   SYSTEM supplies to the management of an organization the data that
195   it requires to make decisions and to exercise control. A REPORT
196   GENERATOR is a program which allows the user to specify in some
197   simple way the content and format of reports which the computer is
198   to produce.
199   To RUN a program is to cause it to be performed on the computer.
200   Running a program to .solve a problem or produce real results (as
201   opposed to debugging) is called a PRODUCTION RUN. Installations in
202   which the user runs his own job are called OPEN SHOPS. Installations
203   which have a COMPUTER OPERATOR who runs the programs for the
204   user are CLOSED SHOPS. Computers are usually operated in
205   BATCH-PROCESSING MODE; the operator assembles a batch of
206   programs waiting to be run and puts them serially into the computer;

207   output from all the programs is returned in one batch. TURN-
208   AROUND TIME is the time between the user's delivering his job to
209   the center and his receipt of the output. TIME-SHARING is a method
210   of operation by means of which several jobs are interleaved, giving the
211   appearance of simultaneous operation. In many time-shared systems,
212   users have individual terminals which are on-line. Such terminals may
213   be located far from the computer; this is REMOTE ACCESS. This
214   allows users to interact with the computer on a time scale appropriate
215   for human beings—on the order of a few seconds between responses.
216   This capability is called operating in REAL TIME. Using the computer
217   for frequent interaction with the user in this way is called an
218   INTERACTIVE or CONVERSATIONAL mode of computing.
219   Like all electronic devices, computers sometimes break down. The
220   prevention and correction of such situations is MAINTENANCE.
221   PREVENTIVE MAINTENANCE finds failing components before they
222   actually break down. RELIABILITY is the measure of the frequency
223   of failure of the computer. During DOWN-TIME the machine is being
224   maintained or repaired; during UP-TIME it is available for normal
225   productive use.

Index

Index

Index